HOW·TO RUN A BUSINESS

WITHOUT *REALLY* TRYING

"This book takes a new and exciting approach on how to teach entrepreneurs. Learning from the mistakes of someone else's experiences will save them from making similar mistakes in their entrepreneurial journey."

—**Daymond John**, TV Personality/Co-Host of ABC's "Shark Tank" & Founder and CEO of FUBU The Collection

"MJ Gottlieb has written a successful book on how to fail--witty, engaging, on the money."

—**Marvin E. Eisenstadt**, Chairman, Sweet 'n Low

"I found MJ Gottlieb's book to literally be a bible- a must read- for entrepreneurs. This should be mandatory reading for anyone thinking of starting a business, or has started a business."

—**Ronn Torossian**, Chairman, 5W Public Relations "One of the Fastest growing Companies in the U.S." – Inc. 500

"With wit, wisdom and tongue firmly in cheek, this book explores the dark side of Wall Street's version of the American Dream. The truth is most businesses fail. It's time someone took a clear eyed and fun look at why."

—**Nelson George**, co-author of *Life & Def- The business memoir of entertainment mogul Russell Simmons*

"MJ's observations are as pertinent to a large global organization as they are to a fledgling entrepreneur."

—**Kevin Hennessey**, Managing Director Senior Advisor, Retired, Credit Suisse First Boston

"A must read for any new or experienced entrepreneur. Full of valuable real-life start-up miscues and insight from someone not afraid to divulge absolutely everything."

—**Bret Mactavish**, Former Senior Manager — International Basketball Operations, NBA

"If I were crazy enough to start a business, I'd read this book first."
—**David Gelber**, Executive Producer, CBS News,
Multi-Award Winning Producer, 60 Minutes

"How to Ruin a Biz provides a method of teaching which keeps you smiling while you tackle the issues the whole way through."
—**Izzy Ezrailson**, Former President, LRG Brand

"A humorous, self-abasing, and insightful guide to surviving the jungle of starting your own business, written by someone who has been there. Should be required reading for all aspiring entrepreneurs--full of lessons and experiences not taught in business school."
—**Scott Shevick**, Former Senior Managing Director —
Bear Stearns and Company, Inc.

HOW·TO RUN A BUSINESS
WITHOUT *REALLY* TRYING

What Every Entrepreneur
Should NOT Do When
Running a Business

MJ Gottlieb

NEW YORK

HOW TO RUiN A BUSINESS WITHOUT *REALLY* TRYING
What Every Entrepreneur Should NOT *Do When Running a Business*

Published in New York, New York, by Morgan James Publishing. Morgan James and The Entrepreneurial Publisher are trademarks of Morgan James, LLC.
www.MorganJamesPublishing.com

The Morgan James Speakers Group can bring authors to your live event. For more information or to book an event visit The Morgan James Speakers Group at
www.TheMorganJamesSpeakersGroup.com.

Please visit MJ's entrepreneurial blog, **www.n2itivsolutions.com**
Contact the author at: **mj@n2itivsolutions.com**

A FREE eBook edition is available
with the purchase of this print book

CLEARLY PRINT YOUR NAME IN THE BOX ABOVE
Instructions to claim your free eBook edition:
1. Download the BitLit app for Android or iOS
2. Write your name in UPPER CASE in the box
3. Use the BitLit app to submit a photo
4. Download your eBook to any device

ISBN 978-1-61448-979-5 paperback
ISBN 978-1-61448-980-1 eBook
ISBN 978-1-61448-982-5 hardcover
Library of Congress Control Number:
2013951386

Cover Design by:
Rachel Lopez
www.r2cdesign.com

Interior Design by:
Bonnie Bushman
bonnie@caboodlegraphics.com

In an effort to support local communities, raise awareness and funds, Morgan James Publishing donates a percentage of all book sales for the life of each book to Habitat for Humanity Peninsula and Greater Williamsburg.

Get involved today, visit
www.MorganJamesBuilds.com

Habitat
for Humanity®
Peninsula and
Greater Williamsburg
Building Partner

"And even in our sleep,
Pain, which cannot forget
Falls drop by drop upon the heart,
Until in our own despair,
Against our will,
Comes wisdom through the awful grace of God."
—Aeschylus

This book is dedicated to all of my failures and mistakes, without which I would never have had the chance to achieve any level of success.

This is also dedicated to the people that told me I shouldn't, couldn't and wouldn't for providing me the added inspiration and dedication to prove to myself that I should, could and would… thank you for helping me turn my lemons into lemon-aide.

The Lemon-Aide Guide is a series that focuses on stories of people and companies who have turned previous failures into current successes, or in more practical terms, have turned their lemons into Lemon Aide!

Why Lemon-Aide?

Shortly after completing my first draft of this book, I was sitting in the chair at the dentist's office explaining to my dentist about the book I had just completed. Being my family's dentist, he knew of my previous shortcomings in the business world. After finishing his inspection of my teeth, he smiled, shook my hand, and while he was walking out of the office wished me luck turning my 'lemons into lemonade'.

Yes, it's true I got the name from my dentist. Thanks, Doc.

TABLE OF CONTENTS

FOREWORD

by "The Shark" Daymond John

I have known MJ Gottlieb for nearly twenty years. Many of the years encompassed the times covered by MJ in this book. Some of the events that took place I was well aware of or witnessed first hand, yet many more I had no idea what he was dealing with. I have to be honest; when MJ first told me about his idea to do this book, I did not like the idea. I think that I remember telling him that, it made more sense to tell people what to do as opposed to tell them what NOT to do. That was my first reaction.

However, he wrote it anyway. I have to also admit that I was not prepared for the emotional rollercoaster that this book took me on. First, I was laughing my butt off. Feeling a little guilty because I consider MJ a friend and it felt a little weird laughing at the pain suffered by someone for whom you care. Then as I started to see some reoccurring themes in this agony, which, was MJ's entrepreneurial trials, I started to recognize some similar occurrences in my personal professional experiences and my smiles turned solemn. I started to nod my head involuntarily in agreement as my memory invaded my reading and I began to relive some poor decisions that I had made in my career that were reminiscent of many of MJ's trials.

I then felt twinges of pain as I also revisited episodes in my professional past in which betrayal of trust was the paramount theme. I also started to feel frustrated at MJ for not being more forthright with me when these things were happening, allowing me to help him when he needed my help the most. Then I came across the case study in the book about being afraid to ask for help and it made a lot more sense. I even found a few more episodes that invoked a giggle or two until I read about another MJ experience that was so similar to my own that my first reaction was that it was referring to me, until it became clear to me that this very painful calamity was not as personal as I had believed. It can happen to anyone and probably does all of the time.

Who knew there could be so much emotion experienced from a reenactment of this glossary of failure? Any readers who are not yet experienced entrepreneurs may just find this book "entertaining" and may even suffer from a delusion that they are "smarter" than the guy who wrote it and/or may feel that many of the warnings are just "common sense" sign posts that any street savvy person would already know and know well.

To a guy like that my only comment would be, "You could be right, but why chance it?" As MJ points out, why exercise a free option? In other words, if someone is going to take the *pain* and go through all of the worst case experiences that many experienced entrepreneurs deal with everyday so that you don't have to, why would you say, "That's cool, I'll make my own mistakes?" To that person I would say that failure has just spotted you from across the room and is working its way through the crowd to personally introduce itself to you. Take this book to heart and enjoy.

MJ, job well done.

ACKNOWLEDGEMENTS

I first would like to thank *my parents* who, though never really understanding this passion inside of me to take the difficult route and do my own thing, have supported my decision every step of the way.

Gary, my business partner and best friend. You have taught me so much not only in how to be a good businessman, but more importantly, how to be a good person. I cannot put into words what you mean to me.

My literary agent, *Mickey "Cowboy" Freiberg*, who never lived to see this project happen. I will never forget you and the friendship we had. I love you and miss you Cowboy.

The king of branding, "The Shark" Daymond John, who has put up with nearly twenty years of my B.S yet never waivered in your support and belief in me.

Skip Prichard, who has been such an incredible inspiration both professionally and personally, and who introduced to me to my publisher, Morgan James, the publisher of this book. You truly live to give with no expectation in return.

My business partner, *John Clomax* (aka "Big John"), who has taught me such a great deal about life and business in such a short amount of time, and who has tirelessly helped me in the final stages of completing this book and for implementing the illustrations to make the book an infinitely more engaging and entertaining experience.

David Belafonte, who, so many years ago, suggested I take my diary of failures and turn it into a book to help aspiring entrepreneurs what not to do in business.

Blogger extraordinaire, *John Paul Aguiar*, who patiently took the time to teach me about the digital space and how to create a blog that people actually want to read.

William Roth, the illustrator of this book who, at twelve years old, should show people that you can't put a restriction on talent due to age, and that anyone and anything is possible when you work hard and put your passion into it.

Izzy Ezrailson, for being such a great mentor to Gary and I over the years. Iz, Gary and I owe you quite a few dinners and one hefty consulting fee.

Gene Nussbaum, who took Gary and I under his wing when we knew nothing and who taught me how to shut up and listen and that an order is not an order until the I's are dotted and the T's are crossed.

David Williams, Mary Michelle Scott and The Fishbowl family who share my desire to help others learn from our mistakes. You are all an inspiration and a living example of how a company can thrive and flourish by empowering and having trust in one another.

Cheryl Snapp Connor, chairman of Snapp Connor PR who, though I have not known long, has shown me a ton of love and support.

My sister, *Jennifer*, for taking the countless hours to manually edit the first version of this book many years ago... on a million hand-written post-it notes.

My brother-in-law and four superstar nephews for taking me away from my business to run around, have fun, and play endless games of basketball until every bit of stress and worry of the day was gone.

My business partner and in house counsel, *Ed Grauer* for always shooting straight, giving the logical answers, never mincing words and always protecting the best interests of our company. You are truly the Mr. Spock of our team.

Jimmy Nulti. You know what you have done for me

All the people who have allowed me to do service to help others. You give me the ability to get out of my head and make me a better man.

PREFACE
Man, Child in a Snake-Filled Land

If, when you were ten years old, you were walking through the forest with your father, and you saw a snake for the first time, how would you react? I'm guessing that you would want to chase it, throw rocks at it, or maybe even pick it up. This is because when you are an inquisitive child, you have not yet learned what to avoid. You are usually taught by your mother, father, sister, brother, aunt, uncle, grandmother, grandfather, stepmother, stepfather, or anyone else who has been given the responsibility of teaching you what is good in the world and *what to steer clear of.* You will learn in this book that when you enter the business world, you are that same child, reaching to embrace every snake that you encounter with open arms. You only need to get bitten once...and you die. Trust me, I know; I've died quite a few miserable deaths.

If you reached for the snake, your father most likely would have told you to steer clear of it, and then he may have given you a sermon on the danger of snakes, how many of them are poisonous, and the potential that snake had to harm you. What would happen, however, if you said to yourself, *"Screw dad's advice, I want to experience it for myself!"* Well, if the snake bit you and he was a good dad, he would probably suck out the poison and take you to the hospital. If, however, he was not so forgiving and the snake was poisonous, you would probably die in the forest having learned your lesson... and wishing you had listened to your father.

Believe it or not, this is the perfect business example. The only problem, however, is that in the business world, once you get bitten, you'll be surprised to find that the doors to all of the hospitals are locked, and they all have the same sign on the front door: *"You should've listened to dad."*

I hope you see the analogy. The *child* is you (the entrepreneur); the *snake* is the challenge in front of you that has the potential to screw you up and set you off course; the *bite* is the actual screwing itself; the *poison* is the debt; and the *hospital* is the bank... So who plays the *father*? Unfortunately, in most cases, the father doesn't exist... but for most entrepreneurs who do succeed, it comes in the form of senior guidance. When entrepreneurs go into business for the first time, they can't draw from experience because any entrepreneurs who are new to the game don't have any. So, if they're smart, they'll learn from those who already have the experience behind them good, bad, or indifferent... So they don't make the same mistakes.

How great would it be if, when we enter the business world, we had that *eternal father* sitting on our shoulder or hiding in our coat pocket, telling us all the right moves to make? Before every decision, every meeting, he or she could tell us, *"Don't do this, don't do that, he's lying ... he's a snake."* Unfortunately, there's no such thing, so learning from the mistakes of others *before* making them yourself is the next best thing.

So who am I, and how and why am I such a great authority to help you? … Quite simply *because I am an expert at screwing up!* Like the vast majority of the greatest and most successful entrepreneurs I have ever met, our greatest lessons have come from learning from our failures. And where do failures come from? If you guessed *experience* then you are catching on! So yes, I have gone through the mistakes, had the failures, hit the valleys, and for this reason, I have become quite skilled in the art of avoiding snakes and, when you do encounter one, how to steer clear from its path. I can even give you some great pointers on how to kill the snake so it never enters your path again. Why? Because, like I told you, I have been killed by several snakes thus far and have learned some invaluable lessons during the process of dying.

You should find this book entertaining (at my expense), as it contains some absolutely brutal, horrifying, and often hysterical tales that, fortunately or unfortunately, I can say are all one hundred percent mine. Almost every bad thing you can possibly imagine in the world of being an entrepreneur has happened to me.

If you are a business owner, just starting a business, or simply have an interest in one day owning your own company, read this book, truly use it, and I promise you that your entrepreneurial war stories (though you inevitably will have a few) won't be nearly as dramatic as mine.

The introduction to this book will assure you that I have the scars to help warn you. I believe that in running any successful business, learning what ***not*** to do gives the entrepreneur the best chance of succeeding, as I have found that many entrepreneurs make the same mistakes, despite the fact that the circumstances leading up to those mistakes may be quite different.

Tony Robbins, one of the people in the forefront of human motivation and success preparation, says two things that have stuck with me that I will never forget. The first is sacred.

> *Success comes from good judgment...*
> *Good judgment comes from experience...*
> *Experience comes from bad judgment.*

The second is equally as sacred...

> *The difference between a successful person and a person that is not successful*
> *yet is that the successful person has more failures on his resume.*
> *The more times you fail, the closer you are to succeeding.*

In the Introduction, I give you a real quick overview of my life as an entrepreneur because I think it's important for you to know about me before diving into the subject matter of the book. I never read a book without reading up on the author first. Without knowing about the author, I feel like a blind man reading, since I don't have a point of reference to help me identify with the experiences leading up to the book, which quite often is the difference between just *getting through* the pages, as opposed to truly understanding and enjoying the experience.

I hope you will find that, by knowing my past, you will understand why I did certain things and reacted in different ways. I also want to show you that I am an ordinary screw up like anyone else, and it took me a while to find my path. A lot of mistakes. A lot. I was the kid that didn't listen to my father and grabbed every snake in sight.

I encourage you, like I did, to make mistakes, make as many as you can when you're young, and learn from them quickly... but there is one other thing you should do that most people, including myself have failed to do... *learn from the mistakes of others.*

If you are an aspiring entrepreneur who hasn't started your business yet, I strongly encourage you to use this as a guide to learn from the mistakes of others before you start your business and the stakes are for real. If you learn from my mistakes, which I have outlined in this book, you should be miles ahead of the game!

One final note...

The actual reason why this book exists is solely based on the result of one particular experience. I'd like to say that it was because I am a tremendously intuitive, genius savant who happens to also be an expert on the psychology of business and how it relates to human emotions, but that simply is not the case. How it happened was quite simple...

I used to play basketball every day at the Reebok Sports Club in Manhattan. Shortly after losing my second business, I started writing all the mistakes I had made in my then twelve years as an entrepreneur, solely for the purpose of getting all of my mistakes out of my brain and on paper as I was in a lot of pain and very confused as to how things went from so good to so incredibly bad in such a short amount of time. One day, a friend of mine, David Belafonte, (the son of the great actor and singer) asked what I was doing so I told him.

He told me that, despite the fact that it was great that I was doing this to help myself get over my business, these mistakes were a potential goldmine to aspiring entrepreneurs and small businesses. He quite matter of factually told me that I could save a world of people entering business for the first time from a tremendous amount of heartache and pain, or I could just continue to be interested in helping only myself. He said, *"Heck, call it everything an entrepreneur should NOT do when running a business."* So I thank David for giving me the foresight, and I truly hope you take the time to learn from my mistakes. If you do, everything I went through will be infinitely more worth it.

INTRO.

To Hell & Back... and the Scars To Prove

When I lost my first business at twenty-six years old, I fell into a deep depression. For the months leading up to that painstakingly difficult process, I drove to the office every day singing the same song over and over again. It was a song I made up called, *"I Got the Two-Hundred and Sixteen Thousand Dollar Blues."* The lyrics were fairly simple and I sung it over and over again to the tune of my B.B. King blues tape on my twenty-five mile journey to the office, which during rush hour on the Los Angeles expressway was sometimes an hour journey at best.

"I got the two hun-dred and six-teen thou-sand-ollar blues and I feel it from my head to my shoes... I got the two hun-dred and six-teen thou-sand-ollar blues dollar blues and I feel it from my head to my shoes..." Over and over and over again. A song I wished never to sing again.

I moved back to New York City broke, miserable, and mad at the world. So there I was at twenty-six years old, business gone, back in the Big Apple, living with my parents, and feeling like George Costanza from Seinfeld. I remember one night I was riding shotgun in my parent's car with my mom, dad, sister, and brother-in-law coming from dinner at Peter Luger's Steakhouse, which was located just over the bridge in neighboring Brooklyn, talking about the one topic that made me cringe...money. Back in high school, my great aunt passed away and left my family some money, which was, fortunately (or unfortunately) divided evenly between my mother, father, sister, and myself. I never valued the money much because I did not earn it, so the only thing I would use it for was, from time to time, to lend the business money to continue to grow. I never really kept track of how much I lent. Ten thousand here, eight thousand there, whatever it was, by the time the business was over...it was all gone.

When I started my first business, I was in my senior year of college. I was obsessed at the idea of running a perfect business. Possessed is probably a more accurate description. I had come relatively full circle and was enjoying the idea of turning a previously frustrating and ignorant childhood into a modern day success story. I worked so hard and so long, my friends used to take bets with each other on the year my heart attack would take place. No one thought I would live past twenty-five. My body had gone from *lean and mean* to *jelly bean*, as I gained fifty-six pounds in the first six months of business. Looking back on it now, it was the ultimate example of not knowing the difference between working hard and working smart. But how I came upon starting a business was even stranger than the obsession I had while running it....

I grew up in an area of New York City known as downtown Manhattan. Ever since high school, I wrote rap lyrics and, after graduating, went to the University of Colorado to play basketball (or so I thought). After getting screwed (for lack of a better word) out of playing for the team because of a coaching switch between my senior year of high school and freshman year of college, I dove back into my writing. By the time I was a junior, I had already made the transition from writing to vocals, and I had successfully recorded numerous songs with the expectation of trying to get signed by a major record label. The name of my group was called *BNW* (*Black 'N White*), and the music was politically motivated, with the lyrics focusing on promoting race relations and fighting the ignorance of racism. The group consisted of only me, since my previous partner, the "B" of "BNW" got the bug to go solo and be a star without me.

One day, after completing a song I was working on, I printed up one hundred T-shirts with the BNW logo on it, and I went to a club in downtown Denver with my best friend Gary and a bunch of other friends. We all walked into the club wearing the shirts and carrying a few more in hand in expectation of giving the shirts away. We went downstairs to see the DJ and get him to play the song. As the night progressed, people began coming up to us, asking us for the price of the T-shirts, and, before we knew it, we had sold the few shirts we had brought. We went to the car to retrieve the remaining ninety plus shirts out of the trunk. By the end of the night, we had sold all of the shirts and had several thousand dollars in cash in our hands. The next day, in the middle of our senior year of college, we quit school and started a clothing business. It was that simple.

Within a few short years, we had a pretty sizable business, supplying nearly a thousand stores. We moved to Los Angeles; got a beautiful office in Santa Fe Springs; a house in Hancock Park, and seemed to be well on our way to success... until it all came crashing down in the process of one single day, when Gary walked into our factory on a routine visit to check on our Christmas production and noticed everything was missing. Needless to say, a half a million dollars worth of uninsured product (will explain later) had been stolen...and we were out of business in a single day.

The next two years were extremely difficult. The first thing I had to do was put the company through corporate bankruptcy to protect myself from creditors. The second thing I did was put myself through personal bankruptcy because I had signed personal guarantees in my business. Then, after getting evicted from both the office and my residence, I put all of my furniture on the front lawn of my house and watched as all the homeless people in the neighborhood came and took it all away. The bank had repo guys chasing me for my car, so I had Gary drive my car to a remote section of Englewood and park it, never to see it again. To make matters worse, after having spent my entire high school and college years making music, I had left my master copy of all the music underneath the passenger seat of my car and forgot to take it before it was repossessed. Nearly a decade worth of original music and tireless effort GONE. I moved back home, severely depressed, embarrassed by the loss of my company, and I told myself I would never get into the business again.

The hardest part of all was moving back in with my parents, as I found it hard enough to look in the mirror, let alone look at my parents after losing the business and all of my money in the process. I spent the next few months walking all over New York City with Gary looking for a job. We knew uptown was the best spot to find a job, but since we didn't have the money for a token for the train or bus, we walked over a hundred and fifty blocks each day, from 20th street to 100th street and back. I told myself that, with the first dollar fifty I made, I was going to buy a token (we had tokens back then) and wrap it around my neck in case the shit ever hit the fan again and I needed a ride home.

We finally got a job together as busboys at a trendy uptown bar on 90th street and 2nd avenue, working for a crazy Moroccan lunatic. Like I promised myself, I took the first buck-fifty I made, bought a token, took the shoelaces off one of my shoes, put it through the hole of the token, and wrapped it around my neck. To this day, I still have never taken it off...and hope I never will.

So I got a job. I went from running a flourishing business to a job as a busboy. Instead of going to the film studios and networks to place our brand on the celebrities on TV, my job consisted of mopping floors. Instead of going to the after parties for the *Soul Train Music Awards*, I was responsible for dumping and cleaning the ashtrays when they were getting full. Instead of managing the five divisions of my company and an account base of nearly a thousand stores, I was monitoring the bathrooms in case the toilets got clogged or the toilet paper needed replacing. And, the most exciting thing, instead of appearing as a guest speaker at a University business class, I was cleaning up the urine off the seats or the puke off the floor after one of the locals had too much to drink.

To make things worse, the owner, knowing my history as a former business owner, would mock me. From the VIP table, smoking a cigar with his fancy suit, Gerry Curls and women in both arms, he would smirk and yell over at me, "*Hey, Fat Mike, The President!* (remember, I had gained over fifty pounds*), someone threw up in the second bathroom...Clean it up!*" The day his bar closed was one of the most satisfying days of my life. I heard he traded the Gerry Curls in for a crew cut and moved back to Morocco because he ran out of money...

As it turned out, Gary and I turned into celebrity busboys if there was ever such a thing. The happy hour crowd would come in after work and end up talking to Gary and I about the business world, or just plain old happy to talk to someone that knew any topic other than sports. I worked every day from three in the afternoon until four in the morning, slept till around ten, and went to *Barnes and Noble* until my next shift started.

I loved Barnes & Noble. I read everyday every type of success story and motivational book I could get my hands on. The story of *Ben & Jerry, Quentin Tarantino, Steven Spielberg, Colonel Sander's* of *Kentucky Fried Chicken, Blockbuster Video's Wayne Huizenga, Sam Walton* of *Wal-Mart, Akio Morito* of *Sony, Phil Knight* of *Nike, Donald Trump, Walt Disney...* you name it, I read it. Furthermore, I read tons of business strategy books... The Guerrilla series: *Guerrilla Financing, Guerrilla Sales, Guerrilla Advertising, Guerrilla Marketing... Swim with the Sharks, The Art of Negotiating, The Art of Business,* and finally, personal development books from *Tony Robbins...* all his works: *Unlimited Power, Awaken the Giant Within, Giant Steps,* and *Notes from a Friend.* Occasionally, I would nod off, and the security guard would nudge me and tell me either I had to keep my eyes open or I had to leave.

Eventually, one customer who frequented the bar offered Gary and I a position in his company renting residential properties, if we passed a real estate course. After about three months, we passed the course, quit the bar, and were at this new job selling real estate in Manhattan. The owner of the bar actually was upset when we quit because we had drawn so many people to the bar. Crazy huh? Two bus boys being the attraction of the establishment. Imagine that!

Anyway, we started this new gig in real estate. I started boxing (I used to box a little in college) with one of the bouncers I knew from the bar and, after being beaten up by him and his six-foot-six, two-hundred-fifty pound frame for about six months, I had dropped the fifty plus pounds I had previously gained. Furthermore, I moved out of my parent's apartment and into an apartment uptown, and I was starting to feel like my old self again. I was ready to get back into fashion and, within a few months, was back in the market as a creative director for a basketball brand. Within two years, Gary and I started a second company, *Entrig,* and I was again back on the top of my game, relieved and proud as hell to be back!

So there I was, a lean, mean, business machine ready for round two of the entrepreneurial world of fashion. This time I was ready! I used my old contacts to bring key people into the company; put the product on hundreds of celebrities; had a great collection designed; talked my way into the best tradeshows in the world; scraped together a few hundred thousand dollars in seed money from investors;

and was off to the races! Before I knew it, we had written orders with over three hundred stores and were scheduled to ship nearly a half a million dollars in our first month! Our product appeared all over television and the magazines, we had distribution contracts in eight countries worldwide, and were well on our way to do over two million dollars in the first year of business. Furthermore, I started to go to all the parties again and loved every minute of it. And I was the President, *El Presidente*, back to the way it was! (Actually, truth be told, I hate titles. Can't stand them. I have never put a title on my business card and never will).

Then it happened again, and it all came crashing down in one single day. To make a long story short, I trusted someone I should never have trusted and left the production of our merchandise in the hands of someone who would later prove to be incompetent. All of the orders from all of the accounts, after nearly two years of preparation in marketing the brand and a worldwide advertising campaign to boot, were cancelled... all because the factory responsible for making the product tried to save some pennies and substitute our denim fabric with a cheaper version without us knowing it, which left us with about twenty-five thousand pieces of useless denim at forty bucks a pop. A million dollar mistake.

The result? No sales; no profit; nothing. All the profits that were supposed to go into paying for the advertisements were non-existent. Suddenly there I was, back in debt, even more than ever before. Thirty days later I was singing a new song... "*I got the two-hundred and twenty-eight thousand dollar blues, and I feel it from my head to my shoes... I got the...*" over and over and over again. I was in bigger debt after two years of the second business then after six years of the first business. Another lesson learned... the bigger the game, the higher the stakes. Better put, if you can't afford *Baccarat*, stick to the nickel slots.

The funny thing is that I lost the second business for the same reason I lost the first business. You would think after suffering so miserably the first time, I would have at least learned never to make the same mistake twice! But that is the nature of the beast (or the biz). Most entrepreneurs get lost in running the day-to-day affairs of their business, and they don't have the patience or guidance to step away from the *war* for a moment to analyze the *battle*. And by the time they do, it is too late.

Book One

MY MOST INFAMOUS
SCREW-UPS...

THE TOP 5 — "THE DO-NOT'S AND NEVER-EVER-EVERS"

#1 Never Ever Ever Spend What You Do Not Have

The Wrong:

When things were growing and looking up for *Entrig*, my second business, my retailers started requesting that my company partake in a national advertising campaign to help make the brand better known throughout the United States. The problem was, however, I did not have the funds to support this campaign. The pressure became hot and heavy from the retailers as they were threatening to reduce the size of their orders unless we took those necessary steps to help establish more of a brand identity. I happened to have friends at the four magazines that we needed to run advertisements in, and I managed to establish credit lines with all four publications and went forward with the advertising campaign. I knew that, with the orders I would be shipping the following month, I would have enough profit built in to pay the advertising bills.

Unfortunately, the factory that was producing our merchandise destroyed the production and all of our orders for the season were canceled. I was looking at a quarter of a million dollars in advertising bills and had only three hundred dollars in the company bank account.

The Right:

When put in position like this, it is easy to be pressured into looking for credit, wherever you can get it from. However, credit destroys ten times more businesses than it helps. And that is a conservative multiple.

Never accept credit without checking with your financial advisors and accountants to see if your company will have the ability to pay the outstanding debts. Your customer will always push you to spend more money to promote your brand. The more money you spend promoting your brand, the less money they have to spend and the easier your brand is to sell. What I did was spend the *estimated profit*. This was highly speculative and extremely risky. Too many things could have *and did* go wrong during the production process. Let me just share a few...

The fabric could be wrong; the boat transporting the garments could have water damage; the shipment could be stuck in a trade embargo; the factory could ship late, etc. etc. etc. All these things could, would, and did happen in my many years of business, and then some. Highly speculative and super risky, indeed. No advisor in this world worth his or her own salt would have given me the go ahead to make such a decision.

Speak to your customers. Establish a personal relationship with them. Explain to them that you are a growing company and ask them if they can help grow with you now, you'll give them concessions later. If you phrase it the right way, they feel well respected. Tell them their loyalty to you in the beginning will earn them your loyalty in the future. You will protect them by not selling to their competitors, you will give them first rights on re-orders, you will choose their store first for in-store signings, radio promotions, and other things of the sort. Give them the real special treatment. And when that time comes, *do exactly what you said you would do.* Then you have a customer for life.

Remember that it is worth more to have forty loyal customers, than four hundred that will drop you the moment someone new comes around. By knowing you have certain customers in your hip pocket, it becomes easier to project your inventory and sales revenue season after season. And when times become tough, you'll be amazed by how you'll suddenly have eighty hands offering you help to get you through those tough times.

Note: This example and the other examples I use in this book apply to all business, and have nothing specifically to do with fashion in particular. Every business has a cost and, while those costs vary depending upon the industry you are in, the principles as it relates to business remain the same.

It also does not matter whether you are product driven or service driven business. If you are in the service business, though you may not have a physical cost of a product, there is a cost to keep providing your service to your customers.

#2 Never Ever Ever Sign Personal Guarantees

The Wrong:

As my first business was coming along quite well, I decided to rent bigger office space on the other end of town. I found the perfect sized space. The warehouse was nearly twice the size of the previous one, and the front office was perfect for what I was looking for. The leasing company required a five-year minimum lease for the space and a personal guarantee on file. Considering my company was shipping several hundred thousand dollars a month at the time, I felt that five thousand dollars a month was hardly a problem, so I agreed to the requirements and signed the lease.

Shortly thereafter, my company was sabotaged during the course of a single day and I was forced to put the company in a bankruptcy position. As I was going through the bankruptcy filing, my attorney realized that there was one creditor who was claiming to have a personal guarantee on file. As we calculated the amount owed to that creditor, I realized I was suddenly responsible for the five thousand dollars for the rent on my office space...multiplied times sixty! I owed nearly five years of rent and was personally on the hook for over three hundred thousand dollars!

Because of this, not only was I forced to file corporate bankruptcy, but also, I was forced into personal bankruptcy as well. At the time, a bankruptcy stayed on your credit report for ten years, so for the next ten years I didn't have the benefits of buying a home or a car, much less a stick of bubble gum unless I was coming with the cash in hand!

The Right:

In this country, the government has granted huge rights of protection for individuals who go into business for themselves. If you form a corporation and go into business, the liability is restricted to the corporation and the corporation only. Therefore, the personal finances of the principals of the corporation are never at risk and it becomes impossible for any creditor to go after you personally because

they are not allowed to break the corporate veil. The only time when the corporate veil can be broken is in instances of unscrupulous or criminal activity within the corporation and/or if the company has failed to pay taxes.

Everyone tries to get a personal guarantee on file, but nobody expects to receive one. There were plenty of other spaces that I could have found where I would have avoided signing this guarantee, however, my excitement and emotions pressured me into making a decision that I ended up paying for dearly.

#3 Never Ever Ever Make a Decision
While in a Negative Emotional State

The Wrong:

The previous example was one of a million examples I have for making stupid decisions while in an emotional state. Here's another one...

One of my proudest accomplishments was being able to consistently negotiate financing contracts with large corporations for the purposes of financing our order book. One season, the company we were under contract with did not accept responsibility for a liability that they had incurred on one of our production orders. I felt so angered and steamed at their negligence that I called their vice-president and got into an ugly shouting match over the phone. Furthermore, I threatened him legally on certain issues in the contract that I felt they were not living up to.

When we finally sat down to discuss the matter in a civil way, we were never able to get beyond the harsh words spoken between us and ended our relationship shortly thereafter. I had destroyed a strategic alliance with a multi-billion dollar corporation because I could not control my anger.

The Right:

When emotions are involved, decisions are made hastily without considering the damage you may be causing for your company's future. Not only did I destroy a lucrative business relationship, but also gave them time to legally prepare their defense as I had blurted out the exact stipulations I would later legally try to get them for. Furthermore, I had not acted in the best interests of my business partners and took matters into my own hands when I had an obligation to confer with them first.

Never make a decision when you are emotional. In this case, from a legal standpoint, if this matter could not have been resolved amicably with all relevant parties present, it would have been best to have my lawyers speak to their lawyers directly, since the emotions would not cloud the facts. The moment you start feeling emotional, take special care not to make a single decision until you free yourself from that emotional state and take the time to truly analyze the situation for what it is.

Do you remember the snake and the father from the beginning of the book? Well, my dad used to tell me to count to ten any time I got mad. I used to look at him like he had nine heads. What in the world is counting to ten going to do, Pops?

It's called restraint of pen and tongue. If you don't have anything nice to say, there will be no benefit in saying it. I used to think putting fear in people was a great business tactic. As it turns out, I was dead wrong. In the end, it leads to nothing but a negative outcome.

... *I should've listened to my father.*

#4 Never Ever Ever Make a Decision
While in a Positive Emotional State

The Wrong:
One day, we had a special guest appear in our showroom. He was a celebrity that I'm sure you would know if you are within twenty years of my age. I was so honored by his appearance that I prepared a free package of clothes for his own personal wardrobe. When I took him on a tour of our showroom, he pointed to a denim set that was on display on the conference room table and he asked if it was his size. I checked and it was! I was so excited it was his size, I packed them in a bag, thanked him, and we said our good-byes.

A few days later, I was preparing for a sales presentation with a major department store. We had recently received some prototype samples that we had been waiting to show them for months, and we were all excited at the prospects of a big test order. The buyer came in, followed by his two assistant buyers, and a few others. I asked them all if they were interested in cold beverages, took their orders and went to the kitchen to get them their drinks.

Halfway down the showroom hallway, I realized something that made me want to jump out our 57th floor window ... I gave the prototypes to the celebrity! I completely forgot why they had been lying on the showroom table that day! Needless to say, we did not get the order, or too many smiles when I came back and told them I had nothing to show other than their cold drinks!

The Right:
Always be in control of your own emotions. No matter how innocent a task you have on hand, always think three times before making a single decision. I must have told eighty people that week not to touch those samples, but you are never

prepared for how you will act when a star walks into your showroom. Also, know that when this sort of thing does happen, they respect you a lot more when you tell them that there are some things they cannot have, compared to letting them walk into your showroom and take whatever they want!

As it turns out, I learned my lesson backwards. About five years earlier, I was at a music convention selling T-shirts and sweatshirts at a concession stand to help promote our brand in the music arena. One of the big female music stars came up to the booth and wanted to buy a sweatshirt. One of my associates told her, *"Are you kidding me? You don't have to pay for this sweatshirt! You can have it for free!"*... I walked over to her and said, *"Forty bucks...don't listen to a word he has to say."* She gave me the forty bucks and said, *"You, I'd hire on the spot."* Then, she looked at my associate and jokingly said, *"You, I wouldn't hire if you paid me!"*

#5 Never Ever Ever Make a Decision While Your Ego Is Involved

The Wrong:
In the waning hours (literally hours) of losing my first business, I sat down with the two gentlemen who were financing my business up until that point. They expressed regret that they could not continue our business any longer. I was literally crushed. For the past six years, I had devoted my life to something that was truly disappearing before my eyes.

They told me that the circumstances that had led up to that decision were too difficult to continue, however they did not question my talent at any point along the way. So much so, that they wanted my partner (Gary) and I to end our company and join them in the initial launch of their new company. We felt slighted. We were not good enough to run our own company so they wanted us to be a part of something else... We made the decision within twenty seconds. No! No! No! No way in a million years! No! ...

Three years later that company would be the largest urban contemporary clothing company in history with revenues now in excess of six billion (with a B) dollars to date. To say that simple, one-minute, hasty decision has cost Gary and I more than a small fortune would be the understatement of the century!

The Right:

Know that most people fail the first time. Also know that most people fail the second time. Things don't always happen exactly the way that you expect them to. In this case, if I had accepted the offer, not only would I have reaped vast amounts of money personally, but also, I would have been able to write my own ticket in the industry for the rest of my career. Once your name is associated with such a huge success, you will forever be in demand in your industry. I know hindsight is 20-20, but in retrospect, it certainly would have been better to take the offer and sleep on it.

2

THE NEXT 5...
THE SINGLE
NEVER EVERS

#6 Never Ever Hire a Friend as Your Attorney

The Wrong:

If you understand the grunts of a new start up business, you certainly understand the need to cut some corners, and cut expenses wherever and whenever possible. I was fortunate enough to have a friend of mine who was an attorney who agreed to handle the legal matters of my company free of charge until I had the money to pay him. Having a growing business, I constantly needed contracts drafted between salesmen, manufacturers, potential licensees and various other employees, clients, and affiliates.

Soon after hiring my friend, I noticed that contracts were being drafted at a snails pace and it seemed the longer and longer I used his help, the longer and longer it seemed anything legally would get done. Before I knew it, his secretary was screening my calls, taking messages, and not giving me any news I wanted to hear about when my legal work would get done. One pressing contract I was waiting for was an overseas distributor's contract to be read and revised in time for a meeting of the minds at our showroom the following month. Upon visiting our office, I informed the distributor that, due to a backlog of my attorney's workload,

I wasn't prepared to sign the contract in his presence. He was so upset that he demanded I pay for his fare back to Germany and related expenses. I refused to pay, and we never spoke again. The contract would have guaranteed over one million dollars a year in orders to our company.

After giving up on my friend after a year of aggravation, I went in search of a new attorney. I was fortunate to have another friend who was an attorney who was willing to take over my legal work. This time it was different. My demands were always met with punctuality and I never had a problem getting through to him when I needed. At the time, I was in desperate need of a very complicated contract. The contract was a responsibility contract within an order fulfillment contract within an overall financing contract. Complicated indeed. The problem was, however, my friend did not specialize in this sort of thing so he would constantly look up information, call other associates and, to his credit, did everything he could to put the contract together.

In the end, as it turned out, he had missed a few crucial points that would later prevent me from collecting nearly two hundred thousand dollars from the party that I was under contract with.

The Right:

In the first example, I was a non-paying client. Whose legal work do you think is always worked on last? Friend or no friend, the non-paying client. Always. Who are the most important two people in your company? You and your partner? Try again... your lawyer and your accountant. It's your job of course to create the money, but if you don't have the guidance to both protect it and direct it into the right places, all your work could put you in a worse position than from where you started.

In my first business, not only did I lose my life savings, but I also lost much more than that from what I made in the years building it. Your accountant's responsibility is to show you how to save the money, how to redirect it from a tax advantage standpoint, as well as how to make that money work for you and grow. Your lawyer's responsibility is to protect that money so all the work your accountant has been doing isn't for nothing. If you don't do this, you might be better off going to Vegas with the money and playing roulette. Would you run off on a horse with saddlebags full of gold without a compass to show you where you are going? Odds are you'll end up in the hands of the enemy.

In the second example, I used a lawyer who didn't specialize in my trade, and forced him into doing something he was ill informed to handle. He did it on time, but it was missing certain key points that were necessary that an attorney who had specialized in that area would have thought of right away.

Simply put... if your business can't afford a lawyer and an accountant, *do not start your business*! Find both a lawyer and an accountant that specializes in your field. In these situations, be careful about *haggling*, as you don't want to be penny-smart and pound-foolish. The rule rather than the exception is, you normally get what you pay for! As my pops says, *"Cheap is dear."*

#7 Never Ever Over-promise and Under-deliver

The Wrong:

After several seasons of aggressively pursuing one of the leading regional chains on the East Coast, we finally received a sixteen-store test order. When asked to quote the delivery dates, we estimated when the product was coming in and gave a March 15th delivery date. Everything was on schedule up until the final week when the factory producing our goods received an order for a much larger quantity than our order and bumped our production for two weeks. After hours of attempted convincing, the factory owner would still not push up the delivery dates, thus we had to settle on the two-week delay. As it turned out, we finished the production nearly on time and managed to ship the order on March 16th.

Several weeks later, UPS returned a huge shipment that had apparently been refused from a customer. When the deliverymen pulled up to the warehouse, they unloaded hundreds of boxes of returned merchandise. I looked on the receiving slip and realized it was from the same chain on the East Coast that we had just managed to ship on time a few weeks earlier. I called the account and they informed me that the merchandise was shipped after the expected delivery dates and the warehouse would not receive the goods even a day after the estimated delivery.

Since it had taken several weeks to go from the West Coast to the East Coast and then back to the West Coast, it was now too late to redeliver the merchandise to another retailer. As a result, we had to eat about fifty thousand dollars that month, an amount a small company like ours could hardly handle.

The Right:

Always manage expectations. In other words, always, always, *always under-promise and over-deliver!*

You know those mail orders that tell you *"please allow 4-6 weeks for delivery?"* Aren't you quite surprised and happy when nine times out of ten the order

reaches you within a few short weeks! They know it'll only take a few weeks, but they are trained to be a hero. They put Murphy's Law into consideration and still add further time on top for good measure. The bottom line is, the customer in my last example would have accepted delivery dates of April 1 if I had given it to him.

The rule is: *Plan early, quote late, ship early.* That way, you're a hero every time… and in the special case that the customer does not accept the quote, it gives you plenty of time to find a customer that will.

#8 Never Ever Sh?t Where you Eat

The Wrong:
My live-in girlfriend was out of a job. She was exceptional at marketing and public relations, so I hired her to work for the company. She did a phenomenal job. She was doing all the things I had expected her to do…and much more. Then one day we had a fight and she didn't pay too much attention to her work that day. The next week we had another fight and this time, it lasted the whole week. That week, she didn't do her job. The next month, we broke up.

For the next several months, not only did I have to take over the marketing responsibilities for the company and look for a new person to replace her, but also had to track all the correspondence between her and our clients up until that point, since she was rather uncooperative to bring me up to speed as to where she had left off.

The Right:
What I had done was a key no-no. A professional organization cannot stay professional under personal circumstances. I had people in my company looking at me with hostility as if I had betrayed them. I got myself in positions where I was uncomfortable, as I knew that I was under close scrutiny. I was told I took favorites and agreed with certain people because of a personal obligation. In retaliation, I started intentionally disagreeing with her to satisfy the others in the office, but then I would get it when I got back home. It got ugly. Never ever ever do it.

#9 Never Ever Teach the Market At Your Own Expense

The Wrong:
In my first company, we decided to take a huge gamble and use a fabric that we had seen in the ski market, and attempt to bring it into the urban market where it had

never been seen before. We decided to premiere it at the biggest fashion tradeshow in the world, the *Magic International Tradeshow* in Las Vegas.

As it turned out, it was a hundred times the hit that we expected. We wrote so many orders we could barely bring the orders physically home. When we got back to the office, we used all of our resources available and managed to ship nearly a half million dollars in orders of these *new to the industry* garments with this specialized fabrication. Day and night we worked shipping the orders until every last order was out of the warehouse.

About a week later, the phones started to ring off the hook. So much so, that we added new lines to take the calls. The reorders were coming in like wildfire. One account with multiple stores in the Midwest called us and told us to ship whatever we had in the warehouse. No discount, just anything and everything we had at full price. *We had nothing.* Not one single garment left. That season, our company rejected millions of dollars in orders because we simply weren't ready.

By the next show we were ready. We went to the show ready for anyone and anything. When we got to the show however, we realized something horrible. Every single booth had our product... and it was better and less expensive than ours was. We were suddenly a zero-factor. A non-issue. The big boys had caught on and were ready for the kill.

Over the next few short years, hundreds of millions of dollars were spent on this fabrication thanks to the people who handed them the keys to the kingdom... Us.

The Right:

This is a classic story of supply and demand. If you have something that someone else wants but nobody else can get, you will get the sale every time, regardless of price. If you're not ready to fill the demand, someone else will, if not now, then later. The key is to reap the most profits as you can until the competition catches on... and they will catch on.

The truth is, we could've probably shipped ten million dollars if we had the inventory. I made a big mistake. I spent all my time on making sure that somehow, some way, the product would be a smashing hit. What I didn't do was figure out what to do once that smashing hit took place.

#10 Never Ever Have Anyone Work for You for Free

The Wrong:

During my second business I had a young woman walk through my door looking for a job. When I told her that I wasn't hiring, she said she would still love to work for the company for the experience of working with a cutting edge clothing company like the one we had.

She started working for us in the marketing side of our business. After the first month or so, she came up to me and asked me if I could simply pay her fare each way everyday from her house to our office and back. I reiterated to her that I told her from the beginning that unfortunately I could not pay anything, even a simple request like this. A week later, she came into my office and asked for the money again in a bit of desperation. Feeling bad, I agreed and covered her personally from my own pocket.

A few weeks later, she asked if I could take care of her lunch expenses while at work. Though this sounds rather petty, we were suffering growing pains at the time, and I literally had no excess money to spend. After saying, "No", she came back a few weeks later and gave a similar desperate plea for the money. Unfortunately, I had to tell her we could not work together anymore.

About a month later, she started showing up in the lobby of our building asking for money to help her brother move back to Los Angeles. Again, I told her I couldn't help her.

A few weeks later, I received phone calls from the young woman threatening that she would go to the department of labor to report we had hired someone and refused to pay minimum wage. It got very ugly.

The Right:

Never fall for this because this story probably happened to me ten times in ten years and always ends the same way. Flip the script for a moment and imagine being that young woman. If you were she and you started working for free, exactly how long would you stay working free of charge? Sooner or later (and most times sooner) you are going to expect your boss to be impressed enough to start paying you. As long as we continue to live in a society that requires money, we can't just live life free of charge.

When someone wants to work for free, there is obviously a secondary motivation. They are willing to work for you for free in expectation of getting paid in the future. If, however, you realistically cannot see paying that person in the future, then don't hire them.

There is an exception to the rule. Hiring students or people just entering the workforce as interns is a different story, and normally works out perfectly. These people need the credentials and experience on their resume, not money. You, the owner, on the other hand, get a free helping hand, and the relationship is often enough mutually beneficial. The best way to find interns is by posting job openings on the school bulletin board as well running ads in the school paper.

3

THE IMPORTANT NEVERS...

#11 Never Write Checks to Cash

The Wrong:
I received a loan from our financing company for approximately fifty thousand dollars to be paid back six months from the date of the loan.

On the exact day the loan was due, I wrote a check back to the company for the fifty thousand dollars that I had owed. The president was out of town, so I gave it to the vice-president to deposit back into their account. He instructed me to rip up the check and re-issue the check to *cash* because the president had owed him the money and, since she was out of town, he would just tell her that I paid him instead of her.

I had a very close relationship with the vice-president, yet I felt very uneasy granting him this wish. After reassuring me there was nothing unscrupulous about the transaction, I reluctantly wrote the check to cash and gave it to him.

A few months later, I was sitting in a meeting with the president, after her return from her trip to China. She mentioned to me that, though she wasn't going to bring it up, she was very disappointed that I had, not only not paid back the loan I had promised to pay back months ago, but also I had made no effort in

apologizing for the delay. With the vice-president in the room, he quickly excused us both and took me into his office before anything further was said.

He told me he had run into personal problems and had taken the money for himself, and that the president did not owe him any money like he had claimed to me months before. He begged me to take the blame until he could give back the money. When I refused, he mentioned the check was written to cash and that I couldn't prove he had withdrawn the money even if I had tried.

Needless to say, I got burned for fifty grand.

The Right:

The rule of thumb is... *never ever write a single check to cash*! It is that simple. Anyone can endorse it, and once that happens, it is impossible to trace.

If you happen to be distributing any cash (such as petty cash), have a log for the person to print and sign for and include the amount given. This accomplishes two things: first, the person recognizes they have accepted responsibility for the money and will tend to be a lot more careful about what and how much they spend because they know they are going to have to account for it later. Second, it doubly protects you in the case such a discrepancy takes place.

In this case, an actual principal of the company that I had written the check to had stolen money from his own company!

#12 Never Be Caught With the Lights Out

The Wrong:

In my first business, the entire production of our garments was manufactured domestically, at various *"chop-shops"* throughout California, where our offices were located. If we received an order, we would find a factory to produce the garments and pay the factory within seven days from the time they delivered the product. We could do this, because all of our orders were factored (a factor is a company who advances you money on your orders), and they would pay us as soon as the retailer received the merchandise. Because of this, we were able to pay the factories in the short period of time they needed to cover their payroll.

We received an order from a large retailer and placed the production at a factory in downtown Los Angeles, where most of these *chop-shop*s were located.

A few weeks before the production was finished, I received a phone call from the factory requesting that some money be paid up front. Since that was not part of the agreement, I refused the request and insisted the factory continue their work until the job was completed.

A few days later, the factory called again and said that if we did not pay money down, they refused to continue. I got in my car and went over to the factory. When I got to the factory, I was surprised to see the factory was pitch black and none of the machines were being used.

When confronting Rosa (the owner of the factory), she informed me that the utility company had shut off the factory's electricity. Because of this, she could not continue and had to send her people home. I could not believe this was happening. This type of thing *only happens to me* (or so I thought). It was too late in the production process to switch to a new factory, so I didn't know what to do…

The result was that I had to pay a rather large electricity bill in order to turn the lights back on and get the workers back to the shop and finish with my production.

The Right:
It is pretty obvious when you go into business that you always check the financial condition of your customer to ensure or at least give you the best chances of getting paid. Sadly, the truth of the matter is that most people forget to check the financial condition of their suppliers and vendors.

When you choose a vendor, you are taking a great leap of faith in that company, and often your entire season can depend on them. Get a company profile on your vendor. If you cannot check their credit on your own, have them give you a statement of financial stability. Ask them for references of clients they are currently doing business with. And make sure you call those references. If they take offense to this, they have something to hide. If they are legitimate, they will not only welcome your questions with open arms but also respect you for your due diligence.

It is also particularly important if labor is involved to ask if it is union labor. Union labor scares the hell out of companies like mine. The last thing you need is a strike in the middle of an important production run. Let me be clear, I have no opinion for or against unions, however I do have opinions about any entity that has the ability to hurt my business. Sit down with the factory and express your concerns. If you are dealing with union labor, ask them if there has been a history of labor problems and, if so, when the last one took place, and what steps are taken when such problems exist. Never in a million years would had I ever paid attention to such a seemingly non-issue, but it happened and it was an issue.

Remember that your supplier is your meal ticket. If they don't do their job for one reason or another, you are in big trouble.

#13 Never Under-Estimate The Importance Of Due Diligence

The Wrong:
A factory visited our offices in New York and gave us a price quote on a denim program for the upcoming season. They had a strong company profile, their

references checked out, and both sides were eager to begin our business relationship together. We gave them production on two rather intricate denim sets, which required a lot of *bells and whistles*, which they had reiterated they were fully capable of handling.

A few weeks into production, we received pre-production prototypes (also called counter samples) to approve for quality and size. Everything was fine with the exception that the stitching was double needle-stitched, rather than the triple-needle-stitching, which was what we had requested. After alerting them on their error, they apologized and insisted the samples had been made in their sample room but would be corrected to triple-needle stitching during production.

About a month later, prototypes were again sent with the stitching corrections. This time, the triple-needle-stitch was present, however, only two of the three lines in the stitching were straight and one was consistently crooked and running into the other two. At that moment, both my partner and I suspected this factory wasn't telling us something.

Though they insisted that everything was fine and all mistakes would be ironed out in production, my partner flew to China and paid a surprise visit to the factory. As we had suspected, there were no triple needle machines in the factory. We had to pull the production from the factory, find a new factory, and start the whole production process over again. Needless to say, by the time the production was finished, we were a month late and suffered over a hundred thousand dollars in cancellations.

The Right:

No matter what business you are in, your supplier's facilities must be visited in person before one penny of business can be thrown his or her way.

In the previous example, the factory was in dire financial trouble. In this example, the financial position of the factory was strong, but the owner was promising to produce something that he did not have the equipment for.

Thus, the third step before giving any supplier your business is, after they show you their financial stability, and after you check their references and company profile...you must visit their location to make sure what they are telling you is the truth!

#14 Never Start Your Business without a Secretary

The Wrong:

It was a week before the biggest tradeshow of the year and I had a million things to do. I came in early and eagerly began to attack my agenda. We had recently increased our advertising coverage, so the phones started ringing early and more frequently that day. During the course of the day, the five people in our showroom had all run out to appointments, and I was stuck answering the phones.

Little kids would call and ask for a catalog. A retailer would call and want to talk to me about the company's history. Stockbrokers would call to try to sell me their newest dot com. Customers would call to book appointments for the show. Potential vendors and factories would call trying to bid on our next production run. By the time I lifted my head, it was seven o'clock in the evening, I hadn't eaten, and I hadn't accomplished a single item on my agenda list for the day... and I forgot to book my plane ticket for the tradeshow to catch the seven-day advance discount.

The Right:

Of about three hundred phone calls received per day, the average business owner would accept maybe eight or nine of those calls. My entire first business went four years without a secretary. My business day consisted of picking up the phone and spending eighty percent of my time diverting phone calls and taking messages, or, simply hanging up on annoying solicitors.

First and foremost, forget about the answering machine. Nobody likes an answering machine. It makes you appear as if you cannot afford a secretary, which, nine times out of ten, is the reality. But if you follow this inherent rule, you'll never have this problem, simply *do not start your business.*

Answering services are worse because the person pretends to be your secretary, which exposes you even more. Additionally, the personable touch is lost with an answering service. Virtual offices say they have solved this problem. To some extent I think they are a good option. The problem, however, is that I want my secretary to have a personal interest in the success of my company, as opposed to the success of the six hundred other companies he or she answers the phones for.

Don't mistake what I am saying here. I am all for being a scrappy, save every penny you can, *eat ketchup sandwich if you have to* entrepreneur (credit to Mark Cuban). What I am saying is that being your own secretary destroys productivity and does not allow you to focus on growing your business, so if

you are putting together some seed money together for your business make sure a secretary is in your business plan. This person will be one of the most valuable people in your company. This person is your bodyguard from the solicitation of the outside world.

Give two lists to your secretary when you start your relationship. The first is a list of the people that, if they call, you will take the phone call *no matter what*. The second is a list of people that you refuse to speak with under no uncertain circumstances.

Then, each day as you come in, write down the names of people that you are expecting to hear from and give them to your secretary. That way, they can get right through to you when they call.

#15 Never Believe It Unless You Can Verify It

The Wrong:
A printing firm had screwed up on a project we had given them which led to leaving a huge gray streak on the side of one of our magazine advertisements. I decided not to pay any outstanding bills until a credit was made to my account.

After much haggling, my account representative informed me that they had applied a $2,500 credit to my account for their mistake. I agreed and paid the rest of the bill minus the credit I had agreed upon.

A month or so later I received a call from their accounts receivable department attempting to collect a balance owed on my account. I informed them that I had received a credit from my account representative. When I told them who it was, they said the person neither worked for the company anymore, nor was authorized to issue such a credit in the first place.

There went another few grand...

The Right:
If you are paying the full balance to a creditor, always write in big bold letters *"Paid in Full"* on the check. Additionally, always have a creditor fax you a *statement of account* before you pay any bill. Make a copy of the statement, enclose it with your payment, and hold onto a copy for your records. That way, the proof is in your hands and not in the hands of a guy that got fired, has no authority, or that no one can get ahold of.

Note: I'm not suggesting that you can not rely on the input of subordinates whose job it is to provide input, just get a decision maker to validate and/or verify the input that you may be relying on before you make relevant business commitments.

#16 Never Put Anything Past Anyone

The Wrong:

In my first business, we had contracted a factory to make our denim production for the season. The terms as always were that we would pay within seven days of the delivery of the product. Once again, the factory owner tried to put the pressure on us and demanded that he be paid on the order before the production was finished. He had money; he was a good supplier, however he was just being an asshole.

This time, I would not concede under any circumstance...or so I thought. I went to the factory and lay down in the middle of the factory floor, blocking both the shipping and receiving docks so no shipments could either enter or leave the factory. I was sure I had him.

He went outside and got in his truck. He drove the truck directly in my path and, as he came within a few car lengths of me, hit the accelerator and floored it. I dashed out of the way shocked out of my mind.

He got paid. And I never did business with him again.

The Right:

If you run any business long enough, you will inevitably have crazy and similar war stories to tell your friends. And this wasn't the first time this happened to me. I once sent my production manager to check on a factory and he came back with a black eye and a bloody nose. Another time, I was followed around an entire park with a camcorder, being heckled and threatened by a Black Panther group who wanted me to leave an event we were sponsoring in the black community simply because I was white. I was escorted out at the end of the day by a team of security guards, not because I did something wrong, but because they wanted to make sure I made it to my car in one piece.

Though these examples seem a tad bit extreme, I probably can tell you five or ten more. You need to understand that, no matter what business you choose to be in, there are people out there who choose to play by their own rules. Many of those people do not do what's morally right, legally right and even criminally right. Those are just the facts.

The moral of this story is to expect the unexpected and to protect yourself at all times. If I didn't jump out of the way of that truck that day, I probably wouldn't be telling you this story. There are lunatics in any and every business and there is nothing that you will do in the course of your business to avoid stepping in the path of a lunatic.

Oh yeah… and don't play chicken with a truck.

#17 Never Use Your Own Money

The Wrong:
As everything was going well at BNW, I would lend the business money from time to time when needed. When sales declined a bit, I would put in even more money to help stabilize company cash flow until sales picked back up. When it was all said and done and the company went into bankruptcy, I had lost not only my business, but also my life savings.

I had a few hundred thousand dollars that I had in stocks that I said I would never touch, but I used that too, so, at the end of the day, I lost everything. I not only lost my house and my car, but I couldn't even pay for a plane ticket back home to live with my parents.

The Right:
Use other people's money. If your business is worth its salt, there are plenty of people, companies, institutions and organizations who will give you money if your company is worth it, whether it's seed money for a start-up, short-term money to blanket temporary growing pains, or long-term investment for company expansion. Furthermore, if your company is either a minority-owned or female-owned business, there are many additional advantages that you can find out by contacting the Small Business Authority (SBA) or your local bank.

Write a detailed business plan on your company, and be prepared to be refused by hundreds of lending institutions and/or investors until you finally find the entity that gives you your chance. If you are thin-skinned and let rejection affect you, you're not the right person to be looking to start a business in the first place. Your first hundred or so rejections are only your welcoming committee to the wonderful world of being an entrepreneur.

If you are one of the people (like I was) who wants to keep the whole pie without having to give up a slice, here's a word of advice… 100% of nothing is worth a heck of a lot less than 50% of something.

The truth is, I never thought the party would end… until it ended. As an entrepreneur, you work to the bone for every penny you make. You want that money to accumulate not dissipate. At the end of the day, when all was said and

done it was like I never had a business. Millions of dollars flew through my account and, in the end, my balance was $0.00 and I moved back into the room where I grew up… and started over.

That quarter of a million dollars that I lost in the first business, if I had left it alone in investments, would be worth several million dollars today. Boo and who.

Note: I want to be clear here on a few things... When I say don't use your own money I am saying your personal money, not the money you have in your business which is completely different. If you don't have money to grow your business, and you don't have the cash reserves or assets in your business to fuel that growth, do not dive into your personal bank account. Somehow, it never comes back. Very few companies on this planet have ever survived without some type of outside assistance. We will dive much further into this in the later chapters...

I am also not suggesting that you should not invest in your business at the start-up level. In the beginning stages of your business, many investors will want to know how much of your own money is in and what you have already invested (your skin in the game). At this stage this is actually admirable, as it shows you believe in what you are doing. The problem, however, is when the business is in full flow and revenue is being generated. At this stage, it is best to take your hands out of your piggy bank and focus on securing financing to fund your growth (We will talk about this in the upcoming sections as well.)

#18 Never Go On a Suicide Mission...

The Wrong:
The beginning of my first business was a truly remarkable and exciting time. One of the largest chains in America, with nearly a thousand stores, had just taken the first urban inspired young men's clothing company in history from twenty thousand dollars to 100 million dollars in revenue and suddenly it was our turn as they were promising us the same future.

After becoming an overnight success from a ten-store test that literally blew out of the stores in a matter of days, we were suddenly receiving orders for hundreds of their stores at a time, and couldn't produce the product quick enough. Our suppliers purchased more and more machinery just to keep up with our production needs.

A few months into yet another large production, we received a phone call from the buyer who was calling to put a hold on her T-shirt order because our in store sales numbers were on a decline. The next day the accessory buyer called to cancel her order for our hats...then the young men's knits buyer canceled our sweatshirts... and finally, the senior VP of merchandising faxed us a letter (there was no email back then) stating all purchase orders would not be accepted by their distribution center until further notice.

As quickly as we had gotten into business, we nearly went out of business... and we never got an order from that account again.

The Right:

Remember the dumb old saying *"don't put all your eggs in one basket?"*... It's not as dumb a saying as you may think.

Always remember to build your own insurance policy in your business. It is much better to have a hundred stores order two thousand dollars from you, than have one client order two hundred thousand. That way, you are not affected by a few canceled orders or if a few of your customers go out of business, or run into financial difficulty.

That event nearly cost us our business. Many of our suppliers were furious at us because they were suddenly the proud owners of expensive machinery that was not being used, as well as unsold inventory from our cancellations. It took us nearly two seasons to recover.

We went on the road and started going from store to store selling our clothing. We attended tradeshows, which would get us thirty to forty customers over a few day time-span, and we started hiring sales reps that had existing relationships with several hundred additional retailers. After a full year had passed, we went from supplying one chain to over two hundred independently owned stores across the country.

We had learned one of the most valuable lessons in business and barely escaped bankruptcy in the process.

#19 Never Grow Too Quickly

The Wrong:
The last story... again.

The Right:
Growing quickly, without a plan on how to implement that growth can be a disaster. In the last example, I was so excited at the prospect of going from zero to millions of dollars; I did not for a second think about the potential downside.

There was actually a specific reason why we got the cancellations and in retrospect, it was a fairly simple explanation.

Our first test order was in ten stores in Colorado. Since we lived in Colorado and had promoted ourselves in the hot dance clubs around the city, everyone knew us, if not personally, by word of mouth. We even knew the managers at the stores we were supplying, and they would give us prime retail space and window exposure at the locations. When the product hit the stores, it literally sold out in a day. This shocked the buyers so much that they started placing huge orders without for a minute questioning why our product had performed on the level that it did... nor did I question it as well due to my excitement and expectation of being a millionaire before I was even legally allowed to drink.

When we received the influx of orders, we should have obviously known that the product was going to many other places other than Colorado. If we had thought for a moment, we would have realized that no one knew about us outside Colorado, and we would need time to promote our product in these other locations before we started shipping blindly nationwide.

At the very point it was too late, I called the senior VP of merchandising and asked him to furnish me a report on our store distribution so I would know where our product was being sold. After receiving the report, I flew around the entire country going to the stores in efforts to meet and greet the managers and salespeople to try to salvage the business and give our company the exposure it needed.

This was way too little, way too late for a number of reasons. First of all, there were too many stores for even a team of thirty people to cover. The stores I did go to however, gave me a shocking wake up call. When I walked into the first store, I went in and asked for BNW (my brand). The store managers told me that they didn't carry the brand, in fact they had never even heard of it. Since it was on my list, I knew it had to be there.

I walked around the store for nearly thirty minutes and could not find my own product. Finally, after thinking I had received the wrong store distribution, I saw a bunch of items hanging on the back wall near the inventory room in between some dress shirts and leather coats. The hangtags on the sleeve were turned to the inside and the graphics on the t-shirts were facing the back wall. Obviously, you can guess whose product it was. I remember being steamed. How can the buyer be yelling at me that my product wasn't selling when their own salespeople didn't even know my brand was in their store and the designs were facing the back wall!

Pretty numbers with a lot of zeros mean nothing without a plan. If you plan to be successful, *learn how to reject a big order* if you are not prepared to handle it. Learning to say NO is a very important skill an entrepreneur needs to master. Unless a merchandising and promotional strategy had been in place before distribution of our product, we would have been much better off continuing to build the business slowly and surely at the ten stores in Colorado, until our marketing caught up in other areas. In addition, the buyers would have respected us in the long term... and maybe we could have been that next hundred million-dollar company.

#20 Never Feed the Hand That Can Bite You

The Wrong:

I had been in negotiations with an overseas distributor for my second company, Entrig, for several months and, after going back and forth on the phone hundreds of times, we finally agreed to the terms and conditions of the deal and set a meeting at our showroom in New York City. The deal would consummate nearly three million dollars in orders over the first season alone, and we were all excited at the prospect of getting the contract finished from a legal standpoint and starting our business together.

As we were preparing for our afternoon appointment with the distributor, I had invited a prospective investor to sit in on the meeting, in an act of good faith to show him I was open to have him witness the closing of an important deal. He came in a few hours before the meeting to discuss a few matters with me regarding his potential investment in my business.

As it turned out, he dropped a bit of a bomb on me that I was not prepared for and asked me for a condition in our contract that I knew I was not in agreement with. I told him we would discuss it at a later time but he insisted on discussing it at that moment. I expressed my dissatisfaction for what he was asking, and, speaking in the best interests of both my partner and myself, I told him, unfortunately, that it would be a deal killer if he refused to let the term go. As the conversation began to get a bit heated, the distributor showed up and we agreed to pick up the issue after the appointment.

The meeting went very well and everything was going as expected. As I would look over at my prospective investor, instead of seeming satisfied as everyone else was, he seemed heated and had the same scowl on his face that he had in our

meeting shortly before. All of a sudden, out of the clear blue he exploded and blurted out at the distributor we were negotiating with, *"Don't listen to a word MJ has to say! He's not a man to be trusted! You'd be stupid to do business with him!"*... He then stormed out.

I sat in my chair shocked out of my skull. The distributor was caught equally off guard as I was and reluctantly got up and told me he was not comfortable moving forward at that time. We never closed the deal and I never got the distributor on the phone again.

There went three million dollars...

The Right:

Negotiations are not the right time to play show and tell. If there is ever a potential deal-breaker in the room, don't take the risk. No matter what the upside, never take a risk like this if the downside can be avoided by simply taking something or someone out of the equation.

When you give someone information, or put them in a room where they can do you harm, your fate is in their hands. Wait until they are on your team before making them privy to anything much less an important meeting like that one.

I found out later, that the prospective investor who had destroyed my relationship with the distributor, later contacted that distributor in hopes to bring him a proposal from a competitor of ours. So much for *good faith*.

4

DON'T...

#21 Don't Jump the Gun

The Wrong:

For Entrig, Germany was one of our most lucrative areas to do business. So much so that I was in the process of hiring a marketing person in Germany to work with our German distributor to help create further brand recognition in that area.

I found someone who I thought was the perfect candidate. His name was Bob. He spoke both English and Deutsche and had residences in both Germany and New York City. Furthermore, he knew all of the important music artists to wardrobe in Germany, which is always the perfect starting ground to expose your product and create brand identity.

At that point, I wasn't ready to have Bob and my distributor talk directly to each other, due to the lesson I had learned from my previous story. I knew both sides needed to know how they would work together, how often they would travel together, what their individual marketing plans were, and how those plans could be implemented collectively.

After successfully negotiating both sides of the deal, I decided I would let Bob and the distributor meet over the phone. After the conversation, both

parties seemed extremely excited. Bob had told the distributor he would meet him in Stuttgart (Germany) the following Monday, where one of the record labels was located. The distributor at the time was on a business trip in Canada, however he agreed to change his itinerary and cut it short to fly back to Germany, and take the long drive from where he resided in Germany to Stuttgart to meet him.

That following Monday night, I received a phone call from the distributor who had made it to Stuttgart. He told me Bob never showed up and never called. He had been calling him ever since but no response. He said he would take a hotel for a few days to wait for additional news.

After two days of calling Bob non-stop, I finally called with a caller id block on my number. He picked up right away, and was obviously shocked to hear my voice! He told me he had missed the plane and was jumping on the next plane the following day. I didn't buy his story since he didn't even make a phone call to anyone, but I decided not to press the issue. I called the distributor and told him he would be there the next day.

Towards the end of the next day I received a phone call from Stuttgart, still no Bob. I called Bob (caller ID blocked) and, again, he picked up the phone. He hadn't left! When I asked him what the hell was going on he replied, *"After thinking it through, I decided not to take the job."* Here he was, after sending my distributor halfway across the world, telling me that he had decided not to take the job!

As you can probably guess, my next phone call was to my distributor, stranded in Stuttgart. He wasn't too happy.

The Right:
Obviously, I should have tested Bob out a bit before sending my distributor halfway across the globe to meet him. When starting any employer-employee relationship (or any relationship for that matter), start light and let them eventually prove to you they are somewhat worthy of your trust. Your customers do the same things with you. They start out giving you a small order. Then, if the product performs, you get a bigger one, and then a bigger, etc. The same rule applies.

Also, again, from the previous story (#20) never put anyone in front of important clients unless you can trust them as much as you can trust yourself. Remember, your credibility is on the line. When I stranded my poor distributor in Stuttgart, he was not mad at Bob (he didn't know Bob), he was mad at me! Bob was representing my company and my company left him stranded in Stuttgart.

I never got an order from my distributor again.

#22 Don't Do Any Work for Anyone Without Knowing Who the Hand That Feeds You Belongs To

The Wrong:
In addition to our business, from time to time, companies would ask us to design collections for other brands (for a fee). One such company approached us and told us that they had acquired the worldwide manufacturing rights for a company who had recently acquired five professional sports licenses. Knowing both the company they were referring to as well as the licenses involved, I felt it would be a rather lucrative opportunity worth a few hundred thousand dollars in commissions at the very least.

I signed an agreement to design a collection for all five licenses, which included an NFL license, an NBA license, a Major League baseball license, an NHL license, and a NASCAR Racing license. I figured I would be better off taking a commission of five percent of the manufacturing revenues on the projected twelve-million-dollar business, rather than a flat fee for the designs.

After approximately three months, I completed all five programs and submitted them to the manufacturer to make samples. The following month, the manufacturer returned from overseas with all of the samples and presented them to the company that held the five licenses. As it turned out, the samples were horrible! The licensing company was so upset; they ripped up their contract with the manufacturer and ended up giving the manufacturing contracts to a different company. Since my agreement was with the manufacturer and not the company holding the licenses, I was shit out of luck...and never received a penny for my three months of work. It wasn't so much about the three months work, but rather the $600,000 in commissions I would have been paid, had the order been executed correctly.

The Right:

When negotiating any contract, always know the source of your income. If your agreement is with an entity that is not the source of the income, or, there is a third party performance contingency involved in order for you to get paid, you are in for big trouble.

In that example, I did my job, however my contract was with the wrong company. While I was confident in my work and was sure I would turn in a program that would be more than adequate, I never thought for a minute that the manufacturer would screw up their work and destroy the entire program altogether.

If you ever do sign such a contract with a third party contingency, make sure you put in a flat fee for services rendered, should such an event take place. That way, at least, you are paid regardless of the outcome.

#23 Don't Be Confused Between Working Hard and Working Smart

The Wrong:

At BNW, I worked seven days a week, and a minimum of fifteen hours a day. If I were lucky, I would get in at seven in the morning and work till ten at night. In the first six months of business, I had gained fifty pounds, was smoking a pack of cigarettes a day, and hadn't done five minutes of physical activity. I had gone from one hundred seventy-eight pounds to two hundred thirty-four pounds, and from a thirty-two waist to nearly a size forty.

There were so many things to do that I didn't even attempt to put them in any sort of planned and organized agenda. I just knew, somehow, some way, and at some point, they all needed to get done. I had an eleven by seventeen planner that I would use to write hundreds of things I needed to do that day. When I ran out of space I would write sideways, up and down, even staple a legal piece of paper to my day's agenda and fill up more and more agenda, literally to the point of driving myself crazy. At the end of each day, if I accomplished fifty things, there were a hundred things that I had failed to do and, without fail, the few things that were absolutely relevant to that day's agenda did not get done!

When ending the company six years later, the business had all but taken its toll on my body, and I was not ready for the devastation of losing the business. Consequently, one afternoon, a few weeks after losing the business, I had to be rushed to the emergency room and treated for a nervous breakdown.

The Right:
Quality works at a thousand times the pace of quantity.

I had a friend who had a tremendously successful business as a hat manufacturer. He had a huge factory with about a hundred or so employees who would all run around the factory like chickens with their heads cut off. All except him. He was always calm, happy, and never flustered. He came in at nine and out at five, took an hour lunch break, and never worked weekends.

Sitting in his office one day, he told me that, at the rate I was going I would never even make it to thirty. He shared with me his key to success. He told me that the key to running a long and prosperous business is to know how to prioritize your agenda, and to never try to conquer the world in a day. His tips were as follows:

Step One: At the end of each month, write your agenda for the following month. Put down every little thing you must do that month, no matter what...

Step Two: Before the first week starts, write down everything that you absolutely must do that week, no matter what...

Step Three: Before each day, write down only the things that you absolutely must do that day, no matter what...

Step Four: Stick to the agenda and always see it through till it gets done....

Step Five: Once your pressing issues are dissolved, just take out the week's agenda and see what's next.

Following these steps keeps the priority of your agenda intact so nothing takes you away from any urgent agenda. There may be only one item on my agenda that day, but you can be sure that would be the first thing I did when I got in. Once you complete what's on your daily agenda, there's no need to work on something else past five when it can just as easily be tackled with a fresh head the following morning at nine.

In business (as in life), you should never reward yourself on the quantity of your time, as it is the quality of your time that counts. There are even times quantity has a law of diminishing returns, like lifting weights. When you lift weights on Mondays and Thursdays, your muscles grow on Tuesday and Wednesday. If you lifted the same muscle every day, the muscle would never grow because when you lift weights, you are ripping and tearing the muscle, and it is only on the days off that the muscle repairs and rebuilds itself stronger than it was before. If you don't give the muscle any time to rest, you will eventually destroy it. The same rule applies in running a business. If you don't give yourself a chance to rest and reflect on the work already done and the accomplishments of the past, you will never regain the clarity and creativity to grow the business in the future.

A few months later, I was watching Mike Tyson in a fight against some fighter I had never seen. From the opening bell, this guy came out throwing shots at Tyson by the dozen. Upstairs to the head, then down to the body, jab, jab, jab, hook, uppercut, jab, jab, jab, straight right...hook! About a minute and a half went by and the guy must have thrown a hundred shots and Tyson hadn't even thrown one. Tyson seemed patient and unfazed. A few minutes later, the fighter threw a real sloppy left hook to try to knock Tyson out. At the very point he thought he was going to connect, Tyson dipped underneath the blow, bent his knees, twisted his hips and threw the hardest straight right I had ever seen in my life...and knocked the guy out cold. End of fight. One punch. So much for quantity.

#24 Don't Be Fooled by Big Numbers

The Wrong:
I had been introduced over the phone to a European distributor through one of my potential investors. The distributor was an importer of large quantities of branded footwear and apparel. After a few short conversations, he asked me to send him samples of our collection as a few of his major buyers were coming into town to visit him. I sent him three samples to start...a sweater, a sweatshirt, and a twill button down shirt.

Upon receipt of the package, he called me with the exciting news that he had received an order for the three samples that I had sent. Seventy-five thousand pieces...of each style! I almost fainted when I heard the news, as the order was over seven million dollars!

After the shock faded and the reality soaked in, I realized that I had a lot of work to do. The first thing I did was to schedule a meeting with our financing company to try to work out the specifics of an order of that magnitude. Second, I spoke to dozens of factories to see who had the production capacity, warehousing facility and the financial ability to handle an order this size. Third, I contacted the popular European media and print publications in attempt to implement a strategic marketing campaign for when the product hit the stores. After that long and tedious task, I finally had everything in place—the financing, the production, the marketing, the whole enchilada.

It took me a few days to get back in contact with the distributor, but I finally reached him on his mobile. He expressed his regret to inform me that, after speaking to his buyer a few days before, the buyer had changed his mind and had decided to pass on the order and would consider the brand again for the following season.

When I got off the phone, I was possibly the most shocked I have ever been. I remember thinking; *"Can he do that? Is it legal to emotionally tear someone's heart from their chest like that?"* I knew the next step would be the most difficult of them all...telling everyone.

The Right:
If something sounds too good to be true... it most probably is.

The first thing that should always set you on guard is when someone waves some huge number in your face with a lot of 0's. That should be your first sign that he or she is full of it. The talkers never walk and the walkers never talk, remember that.

When I look back on that story, there are a few huge question marks that should have popped up into my head from the beginning. First, obviously, I should have done my due diligence on him rather than take the word of a potential investor that he was legit. Second, upon receipt of the samples, the distributor came back with an order without a single question on the particulars. Every buyer asks questions. Any buyer in their right mind would have asked when the delivery dates were, what sizes were available, what colors, etc. A few weeks later, I realized another question he had never asked. I actually had to laugh out loud when I remembered this one.... He never asked the price! Talk about a positive emotional state messing with your head.

All kidding aside, there was a very painful ending to this story. First, the president of my financing company was steamed. She explained to me that she had told the news to her mother corporation in China and would now lose face

(basically, I made a fool of her) in the eyes of their board of directors (they were a public company in China). She was so upset with me that she nearly severed our agreement on the spot. The three factories that we had chosen to do the production told us that they had reserved the factory space and refused outside business from other customers in expectation of our production. All three swore never to accept business from us in the future.... And all the media and print publications thought we were *full of it* when we came back to them a year later for the real thing.

Our credibility had been devastated and, in a small market like fashion, news spreads quickly.

#25 Don't Hide Behind a Phone

The Wrong:
During the BNW years, there were times when we hit financial walls and had to pay everyone late. I had a person who was handling our payables at the time and, he was so flustered by the volume of calls from vendors demanding past due

amounts owed, he put them all through to his voice mail to avoid the calls. He would conveniently call back everyone after six in the evening when he knew none of them would pick up the phone. The situations got worse and worse, as the vendors knew his game and were more aggravated than ever. At the time, I had no idea that such an escapade was going on, as he told me that he returned everyone's phone calls everyday.

Upon finding out his game, I realized he had put our company in extreme jeopardy, as we would surely be screwed if we stopped receiving shipments from our suppliers. I took over his responsibility and jumped in my car and literally drove to every single supplier to talk with whoever was in charge. After a full week of visits, I came back with great news. Not only did I get the dogs off my back, I received extended dating on the current bills until we were cash heavy again. Furthermore, I actually received extended dating (longer time to pay) on all future orders and higher credit lines as well!

The Right:

By taking the time out to see these people in person, I gained a respect from them that I would have never received any other way. Furthermore, by jumping in my car and going to see them, I completely destroyed their previous feelings that they were chasing our company to collect a debt. Instead, I made it so convenient for them to reach me that they had no choice but to work through the issues at hand.

I can probably tell you a hundred other stories like the one above. I have even put out fires simply by showing my face and not even saying a word. By giving your vendor or supplier the *"touch-ability"* factor, they feel much more comfortable to do business with you. It gives them the feeling that you're local and are not leaving town in the near future.

If you find yourself avoiding a situation that you know would better off be handled in person, don't hesitate, jump on a plane, train or automobile and do what you have to do. When you start a business it's like getting married. You have to be with your business through the good and the bad, *no matter what.* If you only show your face during the sunny days, you're no entrepreneur...that I can assure you. And don't have anyone fight your battles for you. The true entrepreneur goes in the trenches and fights his own battles no matter how bleak the outcome may appear to be.

#26 Don't Write Your Own Contracts

The Wrong:
Our financing company needed our permission for their sales force to help sell our holiday collection. Their vice-president came into my office and asked me to sign a two-sentence paragraph that gave them the authorization to sell our product. I had done this many times with them before, so I agreed to sign it, as I felt that the consent didn't require attention from an attorney (which I would have to pay for).

After severing our ties with the finance company months later, the entire product coming in for the holiday was canceled and sent back to factories where the product was made... or so I thought.

As it turned out, shortly thereafter, I received a phone call from a customer wanting to reorder some of the holiday product. Since the holiday season was canceled, I had no idea what he was talking about. I later found out the financing company had brought in our product and was selling it without our knowledge.

We immediately confronted the financing company. They stated that, according to their records, we had turned over authorization to sell the product to them...and they showed the *two-sentence* signed document as proof.

Of course, that two-sentence contract was, under no circumstances, supposed to allow them to continue to sell our own product even without or knowledge, but just to allow them to help sell the line *in conjunction* with our efforts as well.

Since they had a signed document, though not legally binding, it showed that there was enough ambiguity in the letter to justify their thinking of what the letter really meant... and they were not penalized for what they did.

The Right:
During the course of business, I would often come across many situations where I needed to put something in writing, which at the time seemed a bit too petty to involve any legal work.

Over the years I had inherited a collection of hundreds of these little contracts, either that I had written myself, or I had signed without any legal guidance. As it turned out, I got burned in different ways on every single one in one way or another. Possessing a library of the most ignorant one-line contracts ever written had a lot to do with constantly being pressured into making commitments on the spot.

No matter how big or small, skinny or tall, never put your signature on anything until you have the proper legal guidance. Everything can wait a day or two...and don't let anyone tell you otherwise. The same holds true for the other side. They can always wait as well.

#27 Don't Get Overly Friendly With Your Employees

The Wrong:
Jon came on board in January to help us in the marketing department. Things started out fine, as Jon was both a hard worker and extremely respectful. Often, he would come into my office and hang out during lunch. Through the next few months, I would occasionally include him in some key meetings, which my associates were not happy about. Occasionally, I would grab a bite to eat with him, or even hang out after the business day to have some drinks.

As time passed, I began noticing he arrived at the office at around quarter past nine, when he used to come in religiously at the stroke of eight thirty everyday. I would also notice him leaving around four-thirty, when he used to always stay until around seven. I decided to confront him on the issue, and was surprised that when I did, he didn't have the time to talk.

Heated, I decided to let it be for a few days to see if things got better. What I saw next was a further unraveling—increased personal calls, longer lunch breaks, wising off to other people in the office, etc.

I ended it that day.... And lost a great prospect.

The Right:
Unfortunately, kindness is all too often confused for weakness. Though no one ever likes the role of the bad cop, an office full of good cops does not create an efficient workplace.

One of the country's most successful entrepreneurs was being interviewed on television a few years ago and was asked the question, *"What is your secret to your success?"* His answer was, *"always make sure your employees fear you... fire quick and hire slow...that keeps 'em on their toes."* Though this is a rather extreme example and I don't particularly agree with the comment, there is some truth to what he said. I am not in agreement in the least with employees fearing you, but I do believe that you can never lose their respect. Once you lose the respect of anyone, it is nearly impossible to gain it back.

Start by being nice but firm to everyone. For those you feel are mistaking your kindness for weakness, be firm but nice (there's a difference). If that doesn't work, be firm and firm only. Eventually they will get it... then you can be nice again.

#28 Don't Sign Contracts With a Foreign Corporation Unless You're Prepared to Live There

The Wrong:
We decided to sign a manufacturing contract with a factory in China that we thought had the capability of expediting our production process. We spared no expense preparing the contract as it concerned one of the most important aspects of our business. Everything was in the contract to protect us from any foreseen liability, and included all the responsibilities on their side, should they do anything wrong or make any mistakes along the way.

One such mistake they made nearly cost us our business. On one of the shipments, the factory cut all the garments before our production manager signed off on the size specifications. The entire production was worthless, as all the garments were too small. As you can imagine, we had hundreds of stores that were waiting for their shipments for the season, however we knew we would not have the time to rectify the situation since the fabric had already been cut. We were facing several hundred thousand dollars in losses and there was no way to avoid it. Luckily (we thought), our contract had a clause in it that made the factory responsible for all losses. Though this would not help us with the few hundred angry customers awaiting shipment, we were relieved we would at least have financial recovery.

The problem was, however, the factory was not prepared to honor their contract so we had to proceed with the matter legally. As it turned out, my attorney explained to me that, after a bit of investigation (later rather than sooner) he realized that the factory's legal entity was in China, and their office in New York was only a branch and had no legal status in the United States. Because of this, any legal preparation and/or action had to be done in China and we would have to be willing to have a legal team in China represent us through the entire process. Because the financial obligations for the lawsuit were astronomical, and would further require many of our company associates present during the process, we decided to abandon the case.

The Right:
Unfortunately, though I had carefully constructed a great contract with a skilled contract attorney, none of us for a second ever thought of a future scenario like this one. What I should have done was consult an attorney

experienced in international law to see if a relationship could be consummated in the first place.

As it turned out, the long extensive contract was worthless and I had to eat both the cost of the contract and the few hundred thousand dollars in losses as well.

#29 Don't Bang Your Personal Credit Cards

The Wrong:

On one of our tradeshows at Entrig, I had left myself short on company cash and had to use my own personal credit cards to get us through the show. *Us* consisted of eight people. Airfares, hotel accommodations, food, the works. Furthermore, we had union workers building our booth and I had to put my credit card on file in case the labor exceeded the deposit we had made a few months before.

Shortly after the tradeshow is when the roof caved in on the business and, before I knew it, found myself singing that blues song I had desperately wished never to sing again. I was so devastated that I completely forgot that I had used my personal credit cards during the trip...until I got the bill. I was not a happy camper.

The Right:

Remember #17 (Never use your own money)? This is no different. I had never run into this problem before, as I would always have the intentions to pay myself back the moment that I received the bill. But remember, all it takes is once.

When you start a business, take advantage of the many helpful tools you are offered along the way. One such thing is a company credit card. Most credit card companies wait about six months or so before contacting you. They normally go off of a credit report furnished to them by Dun and Bradstreet, which is a company that collects credit information on nearly all American businesses. When you start a business, immediately contact them and start feeding them information on your company. Give them as many references as you can of your suppliers to help them start building your company profile right away. Furthermore, spend a few dollars on their monitoring programs that provide you with up-to-date news on your company credit report and, if there have been any derogatory comments made along the way. Then, the moment you can, get a company card and use it for all company expenses.

A further bit of advice... when you go on a company trip, leave the personal credit cards at home. That way, you are not tempted to use anything else.

#30 Don't Scr?w Your Employees. Literally.

The Wrong:
I did.

The Right:
I shouldn't have.

#31 Don't Act Your Age

The Wrong:
I started my first business at twenty years old. Most of my work during the first six months or so was done over the phone. Soon, however, it became necessary to meet some of the prospective suppliers who would be producing our product for our customers. I set up an appointment to meet the vice-president of the hat manufacturing plant I was considering using for one of the production runs. He picked a spot where he thought would be a good meeting point, as it was halfway between our offices and his plant. It was a quiet little bar in the middle of town.

The problem, however, was I had no idea how I would be allowed in the bar since I was still under twenty-one. Obviously, I didn't want to tell him this, as I felt it might scare him off. I had used a fake I.D. to get in before so I figured I would take the chance. Sometimes it worked, but most of the times, it was refused. I had to take a gamble. Luckily, upon arriving at the bar, it was early enough in the evening that there was no doorman in front, so I managed to get in without incident.

I met the vice-president at the bar, and began talking business. All the time I was discussing my business affairs, I noticed he was acting in a manner very different from the phone conversations that had led up to that point.

A few days later, when speaking with him over the phone, he began to express concern for my financial ability to pay for the production runs. I was quite taken back, since we had worked all these points out over the phone even before we had met at the bar. Finally I figured out what had gone wrong. Here he was that day at the bar, looking at a mere child with no experience in the business, and suddenly he had second thoughts on doing business with me.

That experience repeated itself over and over again during the first few years of my business. As soon as suppliers would see my face, they would go running for the hills, regardless of the conversations that had been made leading up to that point.

On the extreme other side of the coin, one of my partners in Entrig was looking for a job shortly after the business ended around December 2000. He was in his mid-fifties, and wore every year on his face (I feel guilty as I had a lot to do with it). When interviewing for positions, he was being turned down left and right for positions he was even at times, overqualified for. Everyday he would come home tired and dejected from the events of the day not knowing what he was doing wrong and when he would catch a break.

The Right:

In the first example, I was losing my respect at the front door. Every supplier's respect I had gained over the phone leading up to that point flew out the window the moment they saw my face. Furthermore, I wasn't helping the matter any, as I refused and to this day still refuse to wear a suit or any other formal attire for any other occasion other than a wedding.

One day, I took the advice of a friend in the industry that told me to always bring a *gray-haired face* to my meetings, even if that person was to just sit in the meeting and not say a word. I tried his advice one day and it worked like a charm. Furthermore, I found that most of my suppliers were gray-haired themselves and seemed to share many stories in common with the person that I had brought to the table. I obviously was stuck in a few generation gaps, so most of the stories were over my head. As time progressed, I noticed the importance of establishing a personal rapport with the people you expect to do business with. This simple trick opened up many doors that would have been otherwise closed.

After getting my feet wet a bit, I decided I wouldn't let myself be judged by the age factor anymore, and decided that I would confront the issue the moment it appeared, or maybe even before. The moment I would sense the age factor working against me in a meeting, I would stop the meeting to ask a simple question... *"Is either my age or my sneakers going to prevent us from doing business together? I'm here to do business and please let me know if I'm in the right place."* I wish you could witness the 180-degree turns anytime I uttered those words. As most of my meetings started with the supplier on the offense, I switched him (or her) to the defense in one single remark...every single time. They would, purposefully, avoid the issue of age for the rest of our conversation and if anything, would commend me on my accomplishments at some point along the way. Sometimes, I would even take it a step further...

I had one meeting where I knew the owner to have a reputation of being somewhat of a hard ass. I felt that, upon seeing me, it might add some fuel to the fire so I needed to put out the fire before it even started. I walked into the front lobby to the office and told the secretary I was there to meet Mr. So & So. I told her to do me a small favor and mention something to him before he came out to greet me. I asked her to tell him that I was a lot younger than he expected and to prepare himself now so he could gain his composure before he met me. He came out laughing, shook my hand, and we ended up doing business together for many years.

All of these strategic moves I made was for the simple reason of compensating for a situation that I could do nothing about. In my ex-partner's case, the opposite was occurring. He was walking into the interviews wearing the bruises of fifty plus years on his face. As it was, he already had a disadvantage going in, since his best years were *seemingly* behind him. In his case, he could have overcompensated in a different way. First, he should have known the primary issue he was up against and in realizing it, taken a month or two to clear his head and re-energize himself for the future. Second, he had something that I was thirty years lacking... experience (and lots of it). Most of the time, in fact, he had more experience than the person who was sitting across from him.

When you enter a business, know your weaknesses going in and figure out ways to turn them into strengths. There's always a way if you think it through long enough. If you still can't figure it out, read Malcolm Gladwell's, *David and Goliath* and I promise you will figure it out when you are done.

#32 Don't Be Afraid to Ask for Help

The Wrong:
About six months or so after losing BNW, I ran into a friend of mine in the business who had an extremely successful men's brand that sold to many of the department stores across the country. After telling him what happened to the business, he was visibly disappointed, as he was one of our company's biggest fans. He also seemed aggravated at me for some reason, and I asked him why. He told me that he truly believed in our business and would have lent a helping hand to get us through those tough times. All I needed to do was ask, and he was insulted that I had let my pride get in the way of asking for help.

The Right:
In retrospect, there was a point that I had considered calling him, but he was right, I had let pride get in my way. He had always held such a high regard for both my

business and me and I was afraid he would think of me differently. I was not in the mood for sympathy at the time. Though hindsight is twenty-twenty, I remember feeling like an idiot and that I may have had a chance to save the business if I had simply asked for help.

Help, just like misfortune comes when you least expect it and, a simple phone call before closing the doors to the business may have been the difference between bankruptcy and having the business still today. You never know who is your knight in shining armor or when they will appear out of the blue. The following is a story of one such knight...

Just as things started falling into place for BNW, the bottom nearly fell out the moment the mailman delivered a registered mail document to my office. I held in my hands a large manila envelope with the return address of a law firm. This makes any business owner nervous at the very sight. When opening the envelope, the letter stated that BMW, the German car manufacturer was requesting a cease and desist order on all BNW merchandise because our name was too similar to theirs and may be confused by the consumer. My first thought was, how the hell could someone be confused between a T-shirt and an automobile? I knew, however that I needed some serious advice and help, as a company like BMW had the resources to take me to court for the rest of my life…

I needed a trademark attorney, as my general counsel could not advise me on the matter. After calling numerous trademark attorneys who demanded several thousand dollars in retainer fees to even look at the document, I decided to take a different approach. I looked up a trademark firm in the yellow pages (yes, the physical heavy one that hung from telephone booths) and was connected with one of the attorneys in the firm. I told him that I had a legal matter and I would prefer to discuss it with him in person rather than over the phone. Upon arriving at the office, he greeted me at the door. I told him that I owned a small clothing company and had received a document earlier that day that scared the shit out of me (those were my words)…and I needed help.

After eight months of legal representation, we came to an agreement with BMW and I was free and clear to use the logo whenever and wherever I pleased. After all was said and done, I compensated my attorney for the work done.

Who was the attorney and what was the compensation you ask? The attorney was the same one from the yellow pages, and the compensation was a box of free clothing for his children…the only thing I had. The legal work on the case if I was ever charged, was well over twenty thousand dollars, an amount I could never have afforded even if it was cut in half… but I asked for help, and he was someone who was looking to give it. I had appealed to his generous side and he respected me for having the strength to swallow my pride and ask for help.

#33 Don't Introduce One Creditor to Another

The Wrong:

My suppliers would always ask me to keep my eyes and ears open for any extra business I could throw their way, as I knew a lot of people on all sides of the business.

I knew that one of the sewing factories we used for production had many private manufacturing contracts with large retailers and were always looking for mills with any new and innovative fabrics. One day, I decided to introduce the owner of the fabric mill that I was using to the owner of the factory. As it turned out, the meeting went very well and the factory gave them a large order of fabric the following month. The factory also needed an embroiderer to embellish the fabric, and my embroiderer happened to be in close proximity to the factory and I subsequently set up a meeting between them as well. As time passed, all three were doing a fair amount of business together. I have to admit that I felt a bit weird that I wasn't making a penny for bringing them together, however I was happy that I had helped them all out.

In the following months, after a tough season, we fell behind in our payments to the fabric mill. A few days after their most recent delivery, the owner of the fabric mill pressed me further to pay the outstanding bill. Apologetically, I told him I was in a tight cash position and I would pay him the moment I could.

The following day, when arriving at the sewing factory, I noticed that our merchandise had been taken off the machines and replaced by another production run. I could not get to the bottom of the situation, as the owner was not at the factory. Bewildered, I went to the embroidery factory to check on the their progress. When I arrived, I was shocked to see they had halted our production as well.

There is much more to the story, but let me skip to the conclusion... I would later find out that the owner of the fabric mill had called the other two suppliers and convinced them to put a stop on my entire production. Not only would they not continue until I paid the fabric mill, but also I had to pay the sewing factory and the embroiderer their money as well...up front!

The Right:

During the course of any business there will invariably be times when you are late or on bad terms with a few of your creditors or suppliers. This is very common as every business runs into problems here and there. This is why, when you go into business, you should always have two to three sources for everything, so that when your credit lines fill up or you are a bit slow paying one, you can always use the other supplier until you straighten out your account.

In this case, my honesty actually got me into trouble. I had, as a kind gesture, introduced not one, two, but three suppliers to each other who eventually all teamed up against me.

Even though I was paying my bills on time with the rest of suppliers, that one supplier put enough fear in the others for them to change my terms, demand payment up front and threaten to stop doing business with me altogether. That was my reward for trying to help each and every one of them.

Think that's bad? It gets worse...

#34 Dot Every *I*, Cross Every *T*, Leave No Stone Unturned, Believe Wholeheartedly in *Murphy* and Go Over Your Checklist Thrice... and Don't Trust a Soul.

The Wrong:

That is not where the story ends...it gets much worse...

The day the fabric was delivered by the mill to the factory, I was in New York working out of our financing office. I called my partner and asked him if he received the proof of delivery for the shipment. He told me that Harry, the factory owner, had the proof of delivery receipt but he was not at the factory but would bring it in the next day. Though I always made sure we had the proof of delivery on file the same day, I figured that, if for some crazy reason Harry lost the receipt, the fabric mill would surely have a record as well.

As it turned out, since both the factory and the mill were in cahoots against me, and the delivery service was owned by the fabric mill, all parties conveniently lost the shipping receipt and claimed never to have received the shipment. Why were they doing this? They were blackmailing me to pay all their money up front or I would miss my entire Christmas delivery. It gets worse...

I managed to convince my finance company to pay all the charges up front in order to save the season, and I contacted the factory and told them I had the money to continue. Upon receiving the money, they faxed me a confirmation copy of their price quotes for the order. There was a small problem, however. The price quotes were twice what they had previously agreed upon. How could they do this? Let's go further...

Since it was now two weeks before delivery, it was way too late to try to find any other factory to produce the merchandise. Furthermore, the prices previously agreed upon were verbal so there was no proof such prices was ever agreed upon. The result? I was being double blackmailed. I now had the choice to miss the season, which would most certainly put me out of business, or make the deliveries for the season, and make no money. This was not an option either as my overhead was such that I could not go through the season with no profit. It gets even worse still...

I picked the better of two worsts, bit the bullet, and paid the extra cost so the factory could finish the production. When the factory finally completed the production, it was three weeks later, Christmas was gone, and the product was worthless! The season was canceled... and so was our business. Checkmate.

The Right:

Like I said, Dot Every "I", Cross Every "T", Leave No Stone Unturned, Believe Wholeheartedly in "Murphy" and Go Over Your Checklist Twice...and Don't Trust a Soul.

#35 Don't Be Second Out of the Bag

The Wrong:

In Entrig, we were looking to hire a new commissioned salesperson on the East Coast, our strongest potential territory. After interviewing many people, we came across one individual that seemed to have everything we were looking for...and much more. He was currently selling for the top brand in our market, and had relationships with every account we were targeting. Because he represented the top-selling brand in the market, he had the capability of getting us in front of every store we wanted in the first season alone!

I hired him on the spot and he began the following week. After the first month, surprisingly, we had received only one small order. I called his office and his secretary told me he was at a tradeshow in North Carolina. When I finally reached him on the phone, he told me that a representative from the other brand that he was representing (the *top* brand I was just referring to) had been traveling with him on the road. Because of this, he couldn't show any of the retailers our line as he wasn't supposed to be representing any other line and didn't want to get into trouble. As you can imagine, I had a big problem with this; however, he convinced me that the representative would be leaving shortly and he would hit the road with our line the moment he left.

A few weeks later he had a tradeshow in Atlanta, and my partner flew out to work the show with him. At the end of the show, very few orders were written. My partner told me the other brand's line was so extensive and required such a long presentation, the buyers had neither the time nor the energy to look at anything else when they were done.

At the end of the season, hardly any business was written and we ended our relationship with the salesperson.

The Right:
Don't always hire the person with the best resume, as it may hurt more than it helps.

In this case, the salesperson already had a brand that was paying his bills, and had no intentions of putting that in jeopardy. When you have a situation like this and you are second or third out of the bag, neither the salesperson nor the buyer has the time or energy to focus on another brand. Though I received a few orders here and there on the strength of the relationship, my brand never got the necessary attention and distribution it needed from either party to be properly launched.

Again, always do your homework, come with questions, and collect as much information as possible going into any situation. Know how this person can hurt you as much as he (or she) can help you and weigh the scale and make a decision. I was so excited that I had hired the best salesperson on the East Coast, I hadn't considered the potential problems that may occur along the way.

This is not the first example I will give where I found my company second in line. In the upcoming chapters, you will see how the same thing happened to me in the search of an investor.

#36 Don't Gamble on Anyone Other Than Yourself

The Wrong:
I was contacted by a gentleman in Canada named Dan, who was interested in representing our brand in that area. He wanted to arrange a meeting in New York with me to discuss matters more thoroughly. I felt that if he was willing to take the long trip, I would at least grant his wish to see me.

When I met him, I was completely taken back as he was much younger than I had expected. If I had to guess, he was in his late teens. My first feeling was not to take him seriously, as a person such as himself could hardly have any experience in the industry. Then, as quickly as I felt this, I remembered being in his position many years before, being treated in the same way, and remembered how horrible it felt. At that moment, I decided to have an open mind and really pay careful attention to what he had to say.

As it turned out he didn't say much to impress me. He had no contacts in the industry and knew none of the owners or buyers from the stores we were targeting. What he did have, though, was the same hunger I had when I started my business, and I was determined to make the situation work because he reminded me so much of myself.

After making the decision to go forward, my partners second-guessed my decision, as Dan had no experience to speak of, but I stuck to my guns, determined to make Dan a success story.

After about a month, after receiving only one small order from Dan I called him to see what type of problems he was running into. He told me that, unfortunately, his girlfriend had lost her job and he had to take a job until she found work. Furthermore, he asked me if I could send him money for gas and food so he could travel to all the stores in the area until his girlfriend found a new job.

Needless to say, that was the end of the relationship.

The Right:
When you are in a product-driven business, ill-fated decisions like this can cost a lot of money. If you hire a salesperson that ends up not performing, you are in jeopardy of losing distribution in that area for the entire season. This decision cost us a few hundred thousand dollars.

I had gotten overly attached to the situation and sentimental as I saw a lot of me in him. Looking back, however, I remember exactly how hard it was for me to succeed, as so many variables are stacked up against you when you go into a business at such a young age. Bottom-line was, though he reminded me of myself, *he was not me*, and I should have never taken such a gamble to satisfy a personal need.

I would later find out he lived with his girlfriend, had no money saved, and had never quite figured out how he was going to do his job for me, once he got it. I had given him too much credit. Then I remembered a saying that someone once told me...

"Any fool can start a business, but only a few can make money in the process."

5

NO SUCH THING AS...

#37 No Such Thing as... a Cleared Check

The Wrong:
One day, I received a check in the mail from a customer. It was desperately needed and came in at the nick of time as I had about fifty outgoing checks waiting to go out the moment the check cleared. As I always did, I waited the necessary amount of time for the funds to become fully available in order to make one hundred percent sure the money was securely in my bank account.

After receiving notification that the funds were available, I proceeded to send in all the payments to my customers. A few weeks later, I received an angry phone call from one of my suppliers... then another one... and another one... and another one. They were all claiming I had bounced all of their checks! I told them that it was impossible, as there were sufficient funds to cover their checks.

I called my bank to check the balance in my account. I was thoroughly shocked when the representative told me I had a rather large negative balance! As it turned out, the check I had received from my customer had been returned a week after it cleared. I had no idea such a thing was possible.

The Right:

On a check of any significant amount, if you are cash strapped and really need the money, I would recommend taking out the cash you need the moment a check clears and then redeposit it in the form of cash the following day. Cash is always taken as good, no matter what. Once the bank honors the cash disbursement, if the check that cleared is later not honored, it is not your responsibility but theirs. What's more, you can be assured that whatever checks you have written against the cash you deposited will be honored.

The ending to this story gets even worse. I never received a replacement check from the customer. It took a very long time to clear up the matter with my suppliers.

#38 No Such Thing as... a Sure Thing

The Wrong:

Entrig was a bit short on cash for the month, and I desperately needed to pay for the construction on our tradeshow booth for a show the following week.

I contacted a friend in the banking industry and asked him for a personal loan for twenty thousand dollars. I went to him, because I knew he could have lent me twenty times the money if he wanted, and it still wouldn't affect him a bit.

He agreed rather quickly and told me he would wire money into my account by the end of the week. I called the company that was constructing the booth and told them I would wire them the money the beginning of the following week.

The end of the week came, and the money never reached the account. I called his office and got him on the phone. He expressed regret that he had received notice from one of his clients that both he and his partner were being sued for a business matter and unfortunately, he had to hold onto all his money at that time and couldn't help me.

His timing couldn't have been more perfect.

The Right:

After a certain amount of unexplained instances of bad luck, I started using the term, *"MJ's Law"* in place of *"Murphy's Law"* as it seemed everything that could possibly go wrong did go wrong. In retrospect, that is just a fact of business, as unexpected things take place all the time. The truth is, we never think about all of the things that go right, simply because we expect things to go right, and this is quite often not the case. Always have a plan C and D in case Murphy decides to come along on both trips for plans A and B.

In this example, by the time my friend told me the news, it was already too late and I hadn't the time to make other arrangements on such short notice. I was so sure I was covered that I left myself wide open for a devastating blow. You should also realize in this case that, a suicide mission (#18) does not only apply for your customer base, but to all other aspects of your business as well.

As far as money is concerned, it isn't a done deal until the money hits your account and the cash is physically in your hands.

#39 No Such Thing As... A Verbal Agreement

The Wrong:
There was a sales group that worked independently within the offices of our financing company. Though their business was focused on a retailer different than ours, there were a few relationships they had with major accounts that they offered to help us with. I agreed with Matt (the sales group's president) that whatever orders his sales force wrote up, the financing company would produce independently, pay them commissions on, and we would then split the commissions between themselves and us.

Furthermore, they needed our help in designing some additional product (under a different brand name) so that they could attempt to acquire some private label business from some of the other major accounts they did business with. We agreed that those orders as well would be split between the two parties.

After they successfully had written orders on both our product and the product we had designed for them, I spoke to Matt and told him to keep me updated on the shipping status so I knew when I would get paid.

Several months passed, and the Matt informed me that the orders had still not been shipped yet, but he would alert me as soon as they did. Because I was suspicious why the orders had yet to be shipped, I went to the office of the vice-president of the financing company to find out why there was a delay in the production process. The vice-president assured me the orders had been shipped several months before, and that they were in the process of receiving a re-order on the merchandise. Confused and frustrated, I asked the vice-president, *"When will the commissions be paid?"* He replied, *"I paid Matt several months ago when the product was shipped."*

I went back to Matt and confronted him on the situation. He admitted that the orders had been shipped and he had been paid, but he had never agreed to split any of the commissions on the order. He said he thought we were getting our own separate commission from the financing company and that his compensation had nothing to do with ours.

This was a flat out lie, as we both knew there was a specific percent commission always paid by the financing company and it was up to us how we would split the commissions once they were paid. I then confronted him on the product we had designed for him that he had sold as well. He insisted that he hadn't the foggiest clue who had designed the styles and that he had found them lying on the showroom table one day and had no idea where they were from.

Basically, I got conned.

The Right:

Get everything on paper...always.

In this case, since Matt was in the same office as me, I never thought in a million years he would have the balls to screw me and exist in the same office at the same time. I came to find out later that Matt had screwed dozens of people like me and had a horrible name in the industry.

This should also show that you should do your due diligence on not just your suppliers and your customers, but anyone you consider doing business with in any way, shape, or form... and still put it in writing, no matter what.

Book Two

MORE CASE STUDIES AND SOME OTHER THINGS I LEARNED ALONG THE WAY...

6

THE ART OF
SCREWING UP
THE DEAL...

This chapter is dedicated to breaking down and picking apart every aspect and fine detail of securing an investment and getting the deal. This is the starting point of nearly all businesses, because nearly every company needs capital to get started even if it is a small amount. You will learn in this chapter that money is just one of many ingredients of the deal, and that what kind of deal you get often determines the fate of your business before it even starts. You will also learn the difference between *getting the money* and *getting the deal*, and that *who* you choose as your partner means as much, if not more, than any amount of money that is given.

As in the previous chapters, the first section starts with some amusing (& painful) war stories, and then breaks down the mistakes made and the lessons I learned. In this section, I have included all of my failed deals, since each one exposes a different perspective on *screwing-up*.

The second section gives a definitive breakdown on the different types of investors that are out there, and then explains the components and characteristics of each one. You will learn the importance of knowing what type of investor you are looking for, and what types of investors to steer clear of.

The third section gives you a play-by-play game plan of the deal. It will show you how to best utilize your time negotiating a deal, and give you the best possible chance of making your deal become a reality.

Section One... More War Stories when Looking For an Investor

#40 Don't Waste Time

The Wrong:

Our first *potential investor* in Entrig was a man named Jon. One of my associates had met Jon while on a business trip in Canada. Jon was a friend of one of the factory owners that we were currently considering for a small production run in Canada. His company was a large distributor of footwear overseas that bought excess and irregular product and re-sold them in various countries in Europe. His partner was a billionaire businessman in China (so he said), and had the financial ability to fund us the several million dollars we were looking for in capital.

After a few short weeks, Jon asked us to type out a term sheet for the investment and expressed an intention to move forward on the investment the very next week. We were all extremely excited, as it seemed we were finally going to receive the investment we so desperately needed. We were talking to about five other companies who were potential investors at the time, however Jon seemed to be the one who was moving the quickest and expressing the most interest.

Shortly after receiving the term sheet, Jon said he would give us our first capital infusion of $400,000 the following week, as he was just finishing up on a sale and would transfer the funds into our account after he completed his sale.

The following week, I called Jon to touch base. He told me he was just finishing on the sale and he would contact us as soon as it was completed.

Days became weeks, and weeks became months and we still hadn't received a penny. Furthermore, we had lost all communication with the other companies we had been in contact with, as we had been so sure the deal with Jon would be consummated.

We pressed Jon for an answer on the status of the investment. He assured us that everything was fine and that he was flying to China to meet with his partner the following week to go over the terms of the investment one final time.

After another month, Jon returned from China and told us that his partner had decided to pass on the deal.

The Right:
When it was all said and done, we had wasted over seven months on a deal that quite possibly never existed. We had not only given up on the other potential investors we were speaking with, but we hadn't pursued anyone else during that very long process.

What were our mistakes? Well, the obvious one is the suicide mission (#18). You see this recurring time and time again in nearly every example. The biggest problem, however, is the time wasted. Though it is true that you must try and try until you succeed (and will receive a lot of "No's" along the way), you must know the difference between spending time as opposed to wasting it. If you leave the issue of time up to the investor, he (or she) will string you out a thousand times longer than he should, for many reasons.

Though it sounds a bit harsh, treat the investor as if you are giving him the opportunity, which, oh by the way… *you are*. That way, you will operate from strength, rather than weakness. Tell the investor you are not simply looking for money, and that money is not the only qualification for *accepting* an investment.

Section three in this chapter is dedicated entirely to this subject of time and gives you a play-by-play breakdown of how not to waste this most precious commodity.

#41 Don't Spend Time Talking to Ghosts

The Wrong:
Our company ran an ad that we were looking for investors. After a few short weeks, we were contacted by a gentleman named Rodney, who told us he represented a rather large investor who was already successful in the fashion world and was looking to invest in something new. He explained that the identity of the investor had to remain confidential, even to us. Though we found it a bit odd that we didn't even know whom we were dealing with, we decided to press forward in our negotiations.

Over the next few months, we went back and forth many times number crunching, revising projected income statements, and gathering further information for his review. The investor was extremely thorough, as he requested everything from samples to marketing plans, future designs, customer lists, you name it. We took every step and followed every request thoroughly, as we were eager to get the capital and move forward in our business.

One day, out of the blue, we received a fax from Rodney stating that, after final review, his investor decided to pass on the deal...and we never heard from him again.

The Right:
Know the person (or company) you are dealing with. Just as all investors will ask you for your company information, you should ask them about their company as well. If they are against it, they are probably hiding something. Tell them if need be, you are willing to sign a confidentiality agreement so they are protected from you telling anyone else, however you must know who they are in order to begin negotiations.

Any person you disclose information to becomes privy to all your company information. That includes not only your strengths but your weaknesses as well. If they are thorough in their research, it will also include the details of your company, past present and future. Your marketing plans, your future designs, new packaging...everything. In this case, as far as I know, Rodney could have represented a competitor of ours that was trying to see what our plans were for the upcoming season so they could beat us to the punch.

Never waste your time on *invisible investors*. Would you tell your deepest, darkest secret to a complete stranger? Of course you wouldn't. My business fate has been put in the hands of many such ghosts on numerous occasions.

Your chances for getting the investment from an investor you never meet are infinitely small.

Many legitimate companies, however, have a hierarchy that you must pass through in order to reach the head person in charge. Don't confuse this situation with the invisible investor, as the two are completely different. There is nothing wrong with this process and it certainly may be legitimate and worthy of your time. The problem, however, is in these cases, while it is certainly acceptable and expected to pass through such levels, most of the time your climb stops at *the man who reports to the man (or woman)*, and goes no further.

After selling *the man who reports to the man* on the investment, that person will invariably tell you he will attempt to convince the decision maker. He will also tell you that he has a better chance convincing the investor than you do because he knows how he thinks, what to say, etc. The bottom line is you cannot take his word for it. The truth of the matter is that no one will ever have a better chance of closing your deal better than you. If at all humanly possible, you want you, and you only, to control your fate. If you control your fate, and you get the *"No"*, at least you know the best person was pitching the deal and you gave yourself the best shot at succeeding.

There will be many instances however, where you can go no higher than the *man who reports to the man*, as can be the case with large corporations. At that point, you can only hope that person does as well in his presentation to the investor as you have done in convincing him. The good news is, at least you know the investor exists, whereas the *invisible investor* may not exist at all. In the preceding example, since I neither spoke to the investor, nor saw evidence that such a person existed, I have no clue whether or not such a person ever existed.

#42 The Jack of All Trades... Is a Jackass

The Wrong:
We met with a gentleman who represented a large group of investors. He had recently been involved in five successful deals with them, and those deals had outperformed their projected returns on investment. We were happy to know that he was on a roll, and that anyone new he brought to the table would be highly regarded.

As we began our presentation to the group, we instantly felt uneasiness, as it appeared as if we were speaking a different language. Every face had a confused look, and no part of the presentation seemed to be well received. This was extremely out of the norm, as our presentations normally were highly commended at the very least.

As I completed the presentation, there were (as always) many questions from the group. After an hour or so of questions, I began to notice one recurring theme. It seemed that none of the questions were aimed at our company, but were on the nature of the business in general. As it turned out, all of the investments the group had been involved in were in the same or similar industries. The only problem, however, was that they were not in the same or similar industry as ours.

While they all had a comfort level in biotech companies and other companies in the tech space, they hadn't the foggiest idea of how to evaluate a fashion company. Furthermore, as is almost always the case, the only information they had gathered on the state of the fashion industry was what they had read in the papers, which of course, was mostly negative.

The Right:

As you can imagine, our efforts came to no benefit, as the investors couldn't relate due to their inexperience in our industry.

In cases like this one, it is nearly impossible to be successful acquiring the capital or getting the deal. Though it is always helpful to prepare relevant articles on the strength and growth of the industry, if your investors are not informed on the industry coming in, you will be fighting a losing battle that will only waste your time as well as theirs.

If you are an avid follower of the business world, you will see a pattern. Companies that have already reached success, buy other companies in their market. Whether they buy a competitor or invest in a start-up, invariably, they don't stray from the roots of their success. Software companies buy other software companies; telecommunications companies buy other telecommunications companies, etc.

I attempted to win these investors over many times afterward as I knew they had the money to help my company a great deal; however, like I mentioned in the previous chapters, money is only one of many variables necessary in making a deal come to fruition.

#43 Don't Go to an Investor Who Is Looking for an Investor

The Wrong:

My partner and I were introduced to a potential investor who represented a very well known company in the fashion world with revenues exceeding six hundred million dollars per year. After an excellent presentation, we had him excited and eager to continue negotiations. After a few more successful meetings, their vice-president in charge of acquisitions expressed interest in closing the deal as soon as possible. He knew there were investors we were talking to, and he wanted to close on the deal before anyone else had the chance.

Shortly thereafter, out of the blue, we lost all communication with the company. Our phone calls were not being returned, our faxes were going unanswered, and all communication stopped in its tracks. I couldn't for the life of me figure out why...

A few weeks later, my partner came into the office and slapped down that day's copy of the fashion journal. There it was, written in black and white... *Company "So & So" Files Bankruptcy.*

Never in a million years did I expect that one. Bad luck, I guess... or maybe not.

The Right:

As is quite often the case, the bigger a company, the bigger the debt (or its potential for debt). My company was a small company with small debt and, as it turned out, the company we were negotiating our deal with was a large company, with large debt (I owed two hundred thousand, they owed over two hundred million).

This is why it is a must to request the financial information from your investor, just as they will invariably ask for yours. Many people like myself made this mistake and never ask for such information, as I let the fancy office and the glamorous conference rooms fool me!

Always keep up with both your industry trade-papers and the financial publications. As it turned out, in the weeks preceding our first meeting with them, there had been numerous articles in the financial journals projecting their inevitable bankruptcy. If I had known this, I would have never gone through such great lengths in our negotiations.

I guess bad luck had nothing to do with it... just bad preparation.

#44 Don't be the Seventh Man in a Six Man Line

The Wrong:

Our company began negotiations with a very large, well-known corporation with revenues exceeding a billion dollars a year. We met with the president of their sportswear division as well as their vice-president of marketing. They were thoroughly impressed with our presentation and showed an eagerness to continue our negotiations. As weeks passed, and more and more information exchanged hands, both parties showed continued interest in making the deal come to fruition.

The turning point came during the second month of negotiation, as their management expressed to us that there were some potential concerns that may prohibit the deal from moving forward. We arranged a meeting in their New York offices to discuss the potential problems in every expectation of them being worked out and continuing forward.

Upon arriving in the conference room of their New York offices, I realized immediately that a decision had already been made to pass on the deal. The president expressed his regret that their company could not move forward, as they had recently acquired the shirt license from one of the largest denim companies in the world, and they would not have the time or resources to focus on anything else.

The Right:

Had I known going in that they had recently acquired this license, I would have known that it wasn't an opportune time to pitch them the idea of launching a new brand. Though they had plenty of money to fund both, what we needed was a company who was willing to give us the management, the guidance, the focus, and resources necessary to make our brand succeed. Since they had to make a huge financial commitment to acquire such a license, they already had those resources spoken for.

This was yet another lesson learned… that money is only one of many things needed to make a company flourish. If you are the second in line for attention, you quite often never receive it. In this case, if we had been given the capital, we would have most likely been setting ourselves up for guaranteed failure. What we needed more than anything, was a strategic partner to give us the resources, guidance and attention necessary to succeed… and that was already being given to someone else.

45 Don't Pitch to the Designated Hitter

The Wrong:

Our company was in negotiations with a rather large clothing brand in efforts to form a strategic alliance. Our meeting went very well and we arranged a follow up meeting the to discuss matters further. After the second meeting, it seemed that both parties were eager to continue. Then we had another meeting with them, then another, then another.

After about the fourth meeting, I was getting a bit impatient and felt the need to start moving forward legally. I understood that it was a big decision for them as it involved a lot of money, so I exercised as much patience as I could during these long, back and forth *never-ending* negotiations.

The following month, in what I hoped was one of our final meetings, their representative, who was also an owner in the company stated that everything seemed OK and they were prepared to move forward as soon as the owner's brother returned from a trip overseas.

There was one problem. We had never known the owner had a brother! He stated that his brother made all the decisions for the company and would need to be brought up to speed upon his arrival back into the country the following month. I remember saying to Gary, "*Why in the world have we been speaking to a guy who has no decision making power?*"

As it turned out, we never met with his brother, as he was too busy upon his return from his trip. We found out later that the brother hadn't even been told about our negotiations while he was away and never even knew we existed. What a tremendous waste of time that was.

We never spoke to him or his brother again. That was the end of that story.

The Right:
Always know who is sitting across the table from you.

There is a decision-maker in every company and you need to know who that person is before starting any negotiation. Don't ever assume who that person is from the title on his business card, because often enough, it isn't him. A friend of mine is one such decision-maker, as he owns a several hundred million dollar company. His business card does not say Chairman, CEO or President, other people in his company hold those titles. His card simply says his name. Anyone else in their right mind would assume the first three have stronger authority to make a decision, and that is exactly how he wants it.

In this case, I was talking to the brother with zero decision making power, and the guy I really needed to be speaking with the entire time, was five thousand miles away and hadn't ever heard of either me or my company. Talk about wasting time!

If you have been reading this book the whole way through, you should see a recurring theme as it relates to doing your due diligence. In my opinion, time is the most valuable commodity we have and you need to do whatever is necessary to make your time work *for you* as opposed to *against you*.

Doing your homework, knowing whom you are speaking to, and knowing who makes the decisions will save a tremendous amount of time, will increase your efficiency, and give you the best possible chance to secure the deal.

#46 Don't Accept a Boat That Comes With Holes in the Bottom

The Wrong:

We began negotiations with a group that represented a very wealthy man who was interested in investing in a clothing brand. Though he had no experience in the world of fashion (he had built his fortune in construction), he was not afraid at all to get involved in something new. In fact, he had recently attempted to launch a clothing line but was unsuccessful because, though he spent the proper amount of money necessary to launch the line, the individuals he had selected to run the business were incompetent.

This time, however, he was ready to take the extra steps to ensure success. Since he knew nothing about the business and was hoping to learn from his previous mistake, he had hired his own team of *experts* who would be responsible for making sure the company would succeed.

As our negotiations began, I immediately sensed that, though his associates were experienced in the fashion business in general, they had absolutely no knowledge about the market we were targeting. At first it worked to our advantage, as his associates were literally floored by our knowledge on the industry and were easily impressed.

As our negotiations continued further, they decided that they wanted to go forward funding both our company, as well as try to re-launch the brand they had so miserably failed with the year before.

The plans were that our team would run the creative side of both companies, and his team would run the management of his old company, and help with the management of ours as well. Though such an alliance was exactly what we were looking for, we felt that their management was not informed enough on our industry to take part in managing our side of the business and that such an alliance would, if anything, decrease our chances to succeed.

Having agreed on the terms of our deal, we now had to make the decision whether to accept it or to reject it. Though we desperately needed it from a financial standpoint, we sensed that working with their people had the potential to lead to huge problems.

We decided, however, (against our better judgment) to move forward on the deal. After requesting and receiving a letter of intent, we spent a few weeks back and forth with their team discussing plans and strategies for the upcoming seasons. We were so different in these strategies; it was truly amazing why either side had made the commitment to move forward.

As it turned out, a few weeks after receiving their letter of intent, they sent us a fax withdrawing their offer... and we never spoke again.

The Right:

No matter what the upside, know that a small pebble can easily cause a big ripple. The truth was, we knew we had this nagging pebble (their team) yet we chose to ignore it.

In this case, we were lucky they withdrew because it would have been a nightmare had the deal happened. One of the most important parts of a deal is making sure the people you will be working with share your vision. If you sense dissension and disagreement from the onset, you will have a thorn in your behind that will get bigger everyday. Again, remember that money is only one of many required ingredients necessary in the recipe for securing a good deal.

Many companies also go out of business when bringing family aboard too early and it ends up breaking the dynamics of a good company. I have seen this happen a lot. The owner of a business places his spoiled, inexperienced, newly graduated son (or daughter) into the business too early and with too much authority and before you know it, the kid creates enough dissension to bring the company to its knees.

In this case, as it turned out, the investor had found his team in a few aimless phone calls to friends of friends who were in the industry. Since he had neither the time nor the patience to follow the proper steps to look for a qualified team, he paid for it dearly with his checkbook in the end.

When I was the middleman in business deals, I knew both the buyer as well as the company being bought. My job was to make sure that there was a smooth transition such that there were as few ripples as humanly possible. People think merging two great companies together can only lead to one, larger, greater company but that is quite often not the case, especially when people and their egos are involved. Remember AOL/Time-Warner? If you don't, then I suggest you look it up.

It is my opinion that the continuous, seemingly small and meaningless problems, quite often run companies out of business.

#47 When a Door is NOT a Door

The Wrong:
We were in negotiations with a well-known dress shirt manufacturer that was looking to invest in a new venture. They were based out of a town in the Midwest, but had offices in Manhattan. Though they had never ventured out of the dress shirt market, they had plenty of cash and were looking to invest in new brands. After a successful first and second meeting with their President and the vice-president of their New York divisions, they decided to fly out to their corporate offices to see if they could convince the head office to move forward.

Upon their return, the president called me and expressed regret that they did not get the nod to move forward with the deal.

The Right:
Remember #13? In that case study, the factory agreed to produce our order without having the proper tools (machines) in place to execute them properly. This is very similar, only in this case, it relates to an investor that doesn't have the proper resources. You should now start to see a pattern of how this rule applies to almost every part of your business.... and the screw up is all from the same mistake...not getting the information or doing your due diligence in advance. If there is information out there, study your prospective investor thoroughly before you start negotiations.

In this case, if I had studied, I would have learned that the company was one of the most conservative companies in the market, and that never in a million years would they have considered entering a highly speculative part of the market such as ours. I say highly speculative for a reason. The truth is, any investment is highly speculative if it is not in an investor's *backyard* so to speak.

Look back at the earlier example where the investors only had experience in tech markets (#42). Now look at this example and compare the two. Though this company was in the same market as us (fashion), they focused on a completely different customer within the market. Furthermore, despite the fact that they had the cash to fund twenty companies like ours, being from a small town in the Midwest, the mentality of their management was very focused on acquiring a business in their market and their market only.

We simply did not meet their criteria for investment... and no person, business plan or presentation in the world would have changed their minds. There was plenty of historical information on their corporation, which I could have studied in advance proving this very point. Instead, I judged their potential for investment on one single criterion... money.

Though it is true that nothing ventured, nothing gained, you must learn to pick your battles and go after the ones that you at least have some chance in winning. Yes, they were in fashion and so were we... what we needed, however, was a fashion company that fit within our mold. Every house needs a door but not every door fits every house.

#48 The Walkers Never Talk, The Talkers Never Walk

The Wrong:

The president of our finance company mentioned that she was going to introduce us to a gentleman who apparently had the financial wherewithal to give us the capital we were seeking. After speaking with her, however, the vice-president pulled me into his office to warn me about the person that we were about to speak with.

He said he was a man who loved to talk about himself, promised the world to everyone and never delivered. He said that I needed to know this up front, because I would never know this when meeting him. He told me the man was extremely articulate, well educated and impressive, and easily fooled and deceived whoever was in his company. I appreciated his advice, but figured I had nothing to lose. I was also a bit thrown off because the president of our finance company was so sharp and was not someone who recommended people without careful consideration.

The investor's name was Jack and he was a middle aged, very distinguished looking man who owned a liquor distribution company in California. When speaking with him at first, I was a bit taken aback by his extreme downplaying of money needed, as he assured us a million dollars was hardly an issue. He mentioned that one of his partners was an Arab Sheik, another owned a bank, and both were normally involved in capital infusions of twenty million dollars and higher. He was even sharper and more articulate than anticipated and I could see how easy it was to fall for his line of shit...because I had fallen deep already.

After a few talks back and forth, we sent him our business prospectus for him to review with his partners. Upon speaking with him next, he told me he agreed to give me the money that I was looking for, and he would have a bank check available for me the following week.

The following week, Jack called our office and one of our sales people answered the phone. Jack asked to speak to me. When our salesperson asked who was calling, he replied, *"the man who's giving your company a million bucks."*

I found it a bit out of place and tactless to say such a thing, as it was nobody's business other than mine, my partners, and Jack, that such a deal was taking place. I decided, however, to let it go so as not to bite the hand before it fed me.

Weeks went by and I hadn't received either a check or a phone call from Jack. After repeatedly trying him on the phone and receiving no response, I went to speak with the president of our financing company, to ask her if she had heard any word from Jack. She replied that she had heard from him a week earlier and that he had passed on the investment.

He never even called to tell me. We never spoke again.

The Right:

There are certain flashbulbs that should light up over your head anytime you come into contact with someone that promises you the moon and the stars.

The more and more money a true entrepreneur makes, the more and more careful they are on how they spend their money. The same rule applies to their approach to investing, especially when they are considering making an investment in an area that they are unfamiliar with. In such cases, they are usually extremely slow moving, ask a lot of questions, and typically request information about the industry in general from trade publications and other media relevant to that market.

I had previously never witnessed a person make such a quick, hasty decision to spend such a large amount of money. Even if I had, I sincerely doubt such a person would shout it to the world, as such information is often even more private to that person than anyone, and they would not wish any outside person to know such personal information.

I had been warned, witnessed the distress signals, but still was blinded by the sight of a million-dollar check glaring in my face, a glare I actually never had a chance to see on this occasion.

There is one addition to the rule...not only do the walkers never talk and the talkers never walk, but after the talkers don't walk, they invariably *evaporate*... a la Jack.

#49 It's Easier to Dissect an Elephant Than A Flea

The Wrong:

A friend of mine, who owned several businesses himself, put me in contact with a man named Doug that funded all of his businesses. After doing my homework on the investor, I was sure he had the financial ability to provide the capital we were looking for, which was nearly three million dollars at the time. In fact, I would later find out that he could have invested a hundred times that amount if he so chose, as he was one of the heaviest and most aggressive investors in New York at the time. Furthermore, he invested in every type of business you can imagine, from buildings and malls, to movies, Dot Coms, clothing companies, you name it.

His trick was that he would find a strategic partner in each business that had the resources already in place, and would provide the capital necessary for the business to succeed. He was thoroughly impressed with both our initial

presentation and our business plan, so he allowed us to take negotiations to the next level.

As time passed, the negotiations started dragging and the communication became few and far between. Furthermore, it was absolutely impossible to ever get Doug on the phone. I consulted my friend to help give me insight into what steps to take, since he knew Doug quite well both in business and socially. He informed me that, unfortunately, I was one of hundreds of businesses at the time that Doug was looking at, and I would have to wait my turn, like it or not. Furthermore, I learned that he was in the midst of two deals at the time that involved several hundred million dollars, so you can imagine my company's priority was very low on the totem pole.

As it turned out, nothing ever came to fruition with the investor, as communication became too difficult and we had to move on.

The Right:

In the example preceding this one, Jack talked big numbers, but never backed it up. In this example, however, though the investor never spoke about it, he was involved in far too many deals with much lower risk and far greater potential return on investment, and I simply did not fit into his criteria for investment for those very reasons.

Though I had done my homework to make sure he had the financial ability to fund my business, I was quite simply not a large enough fish.

When approaching an investor, you cannot always go by the philosophy that, if you throw enough shit against the wall, something will stick, as you will waste too much time in pursuit of getting the deal.

Section Two... The Many Faces of Investors

As I mentioned earlier, the deal is not only about getting the money you are asking for, but selecting a partner that will give you the best chance of succeeding. In order to do this, you need to know what type of investor you need.

Do you have the idea and the know-how to run the business and money is all you need? Do you need an infrastructure already in place in addition to the money? Do you need money and some senior guidance?

You need to define exactly what you want in an investor before you begin your pursuit of the deal. By having a clear picture of what you want from an investor, you will be much more careful in the selection process so as not to waste any of your time...or theirs. Read the profiles of the different investors and figure out which one best suits your needs...and then go and find them.

The Silent Investor:

The silent investor has one interest, and that is to simply make the investment and hope for a great return. He neither sits on the board nor attends the meetings. He does not meddle in the affairs of the business at all.

This is the perfect investor if money is all you need. Be sure however, that money is in fact all you need. Most companies need a lot more than just

funding. If, however, you feel confident enough and have received some sound advice that money is the only missing ingredient, then the silent investor is the perfect match.

The Loud Investor:

Though he may have no experience in the business, the loud investor wants to meddle in all company affairs. He shows up out of the blue and expects the royal treatment. He makes uncommon demands on the spot; demands free product; wants his own office though he's never there; argues at the board meetings to feel important; and reminds key personnel to remind them where their paychecks come from.

This investor is a dangerous one. It is usually pretty easy to tell these types, as they normally wear their personality on their cuff links. They are cocky, have huge egos, and like to talk about how much money they have.

Some, however are a bit deceptive so it is important for you to always state up front the type of investor you are looking for, and express your unwillingness to tolerate anyone different. I can truly think of no instance where anyone would want to take such an investment. Unfortunately, these investments are very common, as desperate people take desperate measures. As soon as they are in receipt of the money, their own personal hell begins. You would be amazed how one of the biggest and most common causes of a company's demise is dissension amongst the partners.

If your company has to slow down or even temporarily shut down its operations until you find the correct type of investor, don't be afraid to take that step backward. Remember that it is often mandatory to take one step back in order to take two steps forward.

The Celebrity Investor:

This investor is an entertainer, a pro athlete or some sort of high profile individual. Often times, he (or she) simply wants to be able to harmlessly boast to his friends and co-workers about owning a business. He wears the product at media events and tries wherever he can to make the brand visible to as many people as humanly possible. He welcomes the idea of making special appearances on behalf of the company for key events and clients, signs autographs for customers and clients, etc.

This investor is quite often a home run. He isn't in it for the money, but for the glamour of being associated with, and being a partial owner of a business. It gives him a void he can't fill with all the money in the world, as many entertainers and athletes never get a chance to enter the business world until their careers are over. Furthermore, many athletes are stereotyped and considered ignorant to business in the real world and, believe me, many take this to heart. Because of being given such a negative stereotype, many such athletes enter businesses to prove to themselves and others that they are as capable in the business world as anyone else is, if not more.

Their own personal interests aside, they offer a huge plus sign (and more often than not, a huge $ sign) for the company as they give the company a brand exposure that may otherwise cost millions of dollars to create. They also create a further added value to your brand having the ability to attract consumers at special appearances, and other events of the kind.

Remember however, these investors are good only if you need the brand exposure. If you are in a commodity-driven business and selling generic dental floss, such an investor doesn't bring anything to the table other than money.

One word of caution... the celebrity investor can come with an intolerable ego and at times possess qualities even worse that even the loud investor. For this reason, take your time to get to know the person before signing on the dotted line.

The Angel Investor:

The angel investor is a silent investor with good intentions and quite often has valuable contacts. He has resources that he will make available to your company to help it grow and flourish. He may play tennis with the owner of a huge prospective retailer that you have always wanted to do business with, or he may play golf with a banker that can give you the best possible interest rates and terms on a loan. He calls you whenever he feels he can help, while at the same time letting you run your business without meddling in its everyday affairs.

He, like the celebrity investor, has nothing but good intentions to help the business grow. This investor, however, instead of using his status as a celebrity to help the business, uses valuable contacts and relationships to bring added value to your company.

If there is one investor who is in it to help first and make money second, this is the one. His investment may not be a huge one, but it is an important one as many angel investors provide startup capital to help companies get off the ground.

The Strategic Partner:

This is not usually an individual, but an existing company that is either a competitor of yours but on a far larger scale, or is in the same industry as yours with the contacts and resources that you are looking for already in place. They are either looking to acquire a new brand or division, or are looking to invest and participate in a new venture that is a natural extension of their current business, or at least in something that doesn't stray too far from the farm.

This is the partner that most start-ups need but never get because they are too focused on securing cash. What they don't realize is how infinitely more valuable strategic partners are than securing cash alone. These companies are already successful and, the truth of the matter is when a company has gone down the road and been successful once, the road to success the second time is much smoother. It is much smarter to ride shotgun in a Rolls Royce down a well-paved road, than it is to sit behind the wheel of a beat up Chevy with nothing but bumpy terrain ahead of you.

I am a huge believer in strategic partnerships. If you fully understand the resources that strategic partners bring to the table, you should see that it makes a world of sense to go to someone in your market that is already succeeding, and offer them the opportunity to duplicate the process... There is no sense in re-inventing the wheel when it is not necessary.

Remember, at the end of the day, one percent of something is worth a hell of a lot more than a hundred percent of nothing.

The Venture Capitalist:

A venture Capitalist (VC) is usually not an individual, but rather a company. VC's historically act similar to a banking entity in some way, shape, or form. Their qualifications for investment are normally very calculated and cut and dry. If it doesn't fit within their investment criteria, they simply don't make the investment.

VC's normally are not interested if you are a nice guy, or that they believe in you, but whether or not their potential return on investment is worth the risk. Additionally, though they may not require personal guarantees or collateral, they will often want first money back. Understand there is nothing wrong with this, as they are quite often the first money in.

If the startup hasn't provided proof of concept or hasn't gained any traction in the market, VC's will invariably want controlling interest. If they take controlling interest, they have the power in the future to break up your company into little pieces and sell the parts if they think it will make money, regardless of the integrity of your company and its individuals. Remember, VC's look to make their company money first and foremost and if that means using your company to do it, that is exactly what they will do. Again, there is nothing wrong with this, as they are a company like yours. It is up to you to go in with your eyes open or closed.

With this type of investor, it is important to know who you are getting into bed with before even considering pursuing an investment. Should anything bad happen to your business, these investors will own you.

There are times, however, when these investors are exactly what you need. They normally have huge assets and sit on a ton of cash and thus have the ability to make huge investments. In fact, they will not even consider the investment, if too small. If you have a patent or an idea that no one else has, and you are all but assured to capture a certain market that nobody else has tapped into, these guys will give you all the money you need. Most of these investors have been notorious for investing in Dot Coms, techs and similar companies with huge potential upsides.

I must make a disclaimer. Over the past few years, VC's have started to become a bit more human. Some VC's are even starting to switch their criteria for investment and invest because they believe in the entrepreneur more than the idea itself. There are also early stage VC's that specialize in smaller investments as well. My opinion is that it is best to go to a VC when you have something tangible to offer, such as a proprietary intellectual property or if you have enough traction in the market and/or revenue to be worthy of an investment.

It is also good to do some due diligence on the VC before you go to see what type of companies they are investing in. If you are expecting to have VC's sign your

NDA (non-disclosure agreement) my experience is that you will be disappointed. In all fairness, they can't sign NDA's because they normally are pitched so many ideas it is hard to draw the lines between one idea from another... So enter at your own risk.

The Seed Investor:

Seed investors are normally angel investors without the resources or connections. This investor is an individual who is quite often a friend or family member. They have a personal interest in your success and that of your company. Opposite from the venture capitalist that takes a smaller risk on a huge amount of money, the seed investor is willing to take a huge risk on a small amount of money. They are usually part of a group of other family members, friends, or friends of friends that are willing to help your company obtain the start-up capital you need to begin your business.

These investors can be invaluable in the long term for one very important reason. If you can use the start-up capital from seed investors to build strong brand value, the book value of your company may be worth a lot more when its time to look for a second round of funding. By using these start-up funds to get your business going, you may very well be able to go to larger investors when you are ready, and get much more money than you originally planned... and give up a lot less in the process.

Lending Institutions, the SBA, and Minority Lenders

These are all institutions being funded by the government in some way, shape or form. They were set up with the goal to encourage people to go into business for themselves and help expand the job market. Though they all have specific requirements for being approved, they are particularly more aggressive when it comes to female or minority-owned start-ups.

If you have a minority-owned or female-owned business, I would recommend calling the SBA when you begin looking for an investor. You can often find out very quickly whether or not you qualify for an investment. The same holds true if you are not minority or female-owned. The government guarantees a lot of these investments or loans, so the lending institution is more interested in giving you the money than sending you away.

From a time issue, it doesn't take a long time to see if you are eligible, so there is no harm in trying. Remember that nothing ventured, nothing gained.

From my personal experience, these institutions are not great when you are getting started, but they can add good value once your company gets off the ground. Most small businesses have credit lines set up with their local banks to stabilize cash flow.

Another issue to keep in mind is that politics affect the lending habits and spending patterns of banking institutions so the rules can change quite quickly.

Section Three... The Play by Play of the Deal

From the standpoint of wasting time, here is a timetable to help you get the most of your time and reduce any false hopes and/or expectations along the way.

The first trick is to *always negotiate in three's*. This means that you should always have three potential investors on the plate at any one time. When one drops off, move on to the next investor, no matter how promising the other two may appear at the time. Though you should have the full capability to handle three at a time, when you go beyond that number, you start to spread yourself a bit thin and often cannot devote the adequate amount of time and interest to all of your potential investors.

The following timetable will reduce your time spent negotiating a deal to an absolute maximum of six weeks. Since time is the most precious commodity of any business, this will allow you to cut your time significantly in pursuit of the deal. I spent over a year and two months on exactly two deals that led to not one penny in capital. With this timetable, you should be able to go through full negotiations with thirty such investors in the same amount of time that it took me to go through two. That gives you fifteen times better odds at closing the deal.

Step One... The First Contact

When you first contact the investor, your goal is to set up an appointment to meet with them in person. Many investors, however, will ask you to send them a business plan first or an abridged version, like a strategy deck (a PowerPoint or keynote presentation). This is to give them a general idea (broad strokes) of what you are doing, so as not to waste anyone's time on either end. I personally don't believe in sending anything in advance as, nine times out of ten, the plan will sit on a desk or hide in a filing cabinet for months before it is looked at, if it is ever looked at. If, however, the investor makes this requirement it is your call as to what to do. If you

do send something, just know not to hold your breath, as many of your plans will go unread.

There are some instances where sending the plan is ok, like in a private placement memorandum. A private placement memorandum (also called a PPM) is when an attorney that represents your company circulates the business plan to multiple sophisticated parties who invest in a smaller amount of money (called an investment share unit). I would not do a PPM unless you have an attorney represent the investment. If you don't know what a PPM is, ask your attorney and if you don't have an attorney I would drop the subject altogether (for now at least).

Private placement memorandum aside, if you are sending the plan on your own, you need make sure that those plans come back to you, as you don't want any plans ending up in the wrong person's hands.

Step Two... Sending the Plan

When you send the plan, have a place for the potential investor's name, and number the plan on the opening page. The reasons for doing this are twofold. First, if there is no interest, the plan is returned and re-circulated. By knowing which number corresponds to which investor, you can always call to get the plan back if it hasn't been returned. Secondly, it shows the investor that he or she is not the only person being given *the opportunity* to invest. Make sure, however, you start numbering at around "23" so, in the case you have sent out only one plan, your investor doesn't think he's the only game in town (a useful trick on hiding weakness and showing strength).

Furthermore, include a small paragraph under the plan number. This paragraph should state four simple things: First, it should state that the plan is given in confidentiality and is intended for the recipient only. Second, a request that the plan be reviewed within a time period of two weeks. Third, if after that time period there is no interest, contact the office of the sender so that arrangements are made for the plan to be either picked up or overnighted back the following business day. Fourth, if the plan has been received by anyone else other than the intended recipient, to please contact the sender immediately (& include phone and address) to make arrangements for the plan to be returned.

Step Three... The Letter

When sending the plan, include a letter to the recipients thanking them for their interest in your company. Thank them in advance for their careful time and consideration reviewing the proposal, and respectfully asking *(not telling)* them to take every bit of the two weeks to review, but to please respect the time allotted for a decision whether good, bad or indifferent.

If you know the company or person personally, include a personal touch. This is very important...if you know he's a tennis player, mention a match that happened recently in the papers. If you know his daughter is studying for midterms, wish his daughter luck in her studies, etc., etc. You'd be surprised how the personal touch sometimes can be the difference between an investor reading your prospectus right away, or putting it in his drawer and ignoring your request for a quick response.

Know the difference however, between putting in a personal note like this (a strength) and kissing ass (a huge weakness)! If you don't know the difference, read the letter to a trusted friend or associate and he or she will tell you right away whether you are kissing ass or just being smart. Finally, conclude by stating that you will follow up in a week's time to answer any questions or concerns he had gained along the way.

Step Four... The Follow-up Call

When making the follow-up call, remember, you told him in the letter you would give him the two weeks so don't ask him what he thought of your prospectus. You are calling him simply to touch base and to see if he has any questions. Finish by telling him you'll speak to him in a week's time to discuss further. Then leave him alone for that final week.

This is an important conversation for a few key reasons. First, if he tells you he hasn't had a chance yet to review the plan, you are *reminding him* that you need an answer one way or another the following week. Do not be afraid to do this as, if not he can (and most probably will) take forever. If he is a true businessman, he will understand the importance of time, and will respect your request to not waste it on either end. Furthermore, it will get your business plan to the head of the line, in front of all the other plans that did not have a time limit for review.

Step Five... The Two-Week Call

After the two weeks are up, call the investor to ask what his feelings are and whether or not he has an interest moving forward.

If his answer is "No" and he has chosen to pass, thank him for his time and consideration, and his prompt response. Ask (not tell) him, if he can share with you the reason(s) for passing on the deal...this is super important. Now that you have received the "No," knowing the *why* may help you considerably for your next investor and give yourself time to revise the plan if necessary. You must learn what you may have done wrong in order to have a better chance at getting it right the next time. Remember to never burn bridges.

Second, and equally as important, ask him whom he may know who may be interested. You would be surprised how this often leads you to the investor you are looking for. Remember that people who have money hang out with other people who have money. If your proposal may not be right for them, it may very well be perfect for their doubles partner at the country club. Remember, one man's trash is another man's treasure.

Now you need to tell him to send the plan back, unless he is planning to pass it off to someone else. If it is a flat "No" tell him you will schedule Fed Ex to pick up the plan from him. Yes you need a Fed Ex or UPS account in order to get your plans back. If you leave it up to him you probably won't get it back and if you don't trust the person with your shipping account number, you should not have sent him the plan in the first place. Finish by sending him a letter expressing the same gratitude for his quick review and prompt response.

If his response is to continue further discussion, setup the appointment on the spot. Make the appointment as early as possible so you are fresh in his mind. You don't want to give him any added time to back out and change his mind.

If he hasn't yet reviewed the plan, or he needs a bit more time for review, give him a week and a week only. If you call and his secretary says he is out of town, or unavailable, kindly tell them you will send someone the following day to pick up the plan. You will be surprised how, more often than not, you receive a call before the day is out with a response one-way or the other.

Step Six... The Meeting of the Minds

When meeting the investor(s), always give a firm handshake. Undoubtedly, you've heard this before, as it does work. It shows confidence and power, which are two very significant leverage points in every deal.

Conduct the meeting to the best of your ability, and remember to operate from strength at all times. Make them feel quite comfortable but still make sure they know you are reviewing them in the same way that they are reviewing you. Just as he will have questions for you, you should have questions for him.

Conclude the meeting in a similar fashion that you concluded the letter sent with the business plan. Tell them to take a week to review the points discussed, and that if all parties are willing to take it to the next step, you will set up a second meeting to discuss the specifics the following week.

Step Seven...The Post-Meeting Report

If the answer is "No" follow the same steps as before.

If they say they are interested but need more time to consider the investment, I would not give them longer than a week to consider the deal. The more space you put between each meeting, the lower your chances are to getting the next one. They must know you have other people looking at the investment, without you having to publicly announce it.

If the answer is "Yes" to continue further discussions, again, follow the same step as before and make the appointment immediately. Your conversation now should be getting more specific. Because of this, you need to start moving to your deal points. Ask them what questions, issues or concerns they may have, so you are prepared to address them at the next meeting.

Step Eight... The Number Crunching Meeting

Crunch the numbers, answer the questions, and make sure everyone is informed and on the same page. Once the meeting is finished, see if everyone is in agreement with the terms and conditions discussed. If everyone is on the same page, it is sometimes wise to ask them for a *letter of intent* stating both their intent and the terms and conditions of the deal, as they understand it. The letter of intent legally means nothing, but accomplishes many things for both the investors and any other investor you may be in negotiations with at the time.

When you receive the letter, you have added a key leverage point in your negotiations with anyone else you may be negotiating with at the time. Send a notification out to all of the other potential investors letting them know that you have received a letter of intent. You are doing this both out of courtesy as well as to give them a chance to come in on the offer.

Step Nine... Bring in the Lawyers

Once in receipt of the letter of intent, if you are in agreement with the terms and conditions they have stated, ask for their permission to move forward and enter the legal process. Have the contract ready as fast as humanly possible and deliver the contract priority overnight once you have completed it. You should have already worked out the terms with your lawyer so there should only be modifications to an agreement that is already in place.

Make sure the lawyer you have selected is a *deal-maker* and not a *deal-killer*.

Selecting the right lawyer is much more important than you may think, as they are the final step before closing any deal. If you have a confrontational or overly opinionated lawyer you are digging your own grave, and all the work and time you put in to get to that point will have been for naught. If anything, you want a lawyer that will further increase your chances of closing the deal.

As difficult as this may seem to accept (as I have said before), 1% of a large pie can be worth infinitely more than 100% of a small pie and all too often we are confronted with the dilemma of this choice when there seems to be no one else with the passion and/or financing to help us achieve our business goals. Do not allow the comfort of your *hopes and dreams* seduce you away from the starkness of hardcore business reality. Hire a deal-maker.

When closing the deal, be friendly but not overly friendly, and stick to business until the contracts are signed. Do not get overexcited. Though you may feel you have just won the lottery, if you have done your job correctly, you have made them feel as if they won the lottery as well.

A good negotiation has a mutually beneficial result *or Win-Win. I win because you win.*

Note: *A deal-maker is a lawyer who understands the difference between a business decision and an inferior legal position. He will advise you on pertinent business issues but protect you on critical legal issues. Whatever business decisions that you have made, he implements them while protecting you legally.*

A deal-killer is a lawyer who does not give advice, as much as gives direction. He (or she) is typically negative about how the deal should be done. Remember, legal concerns are why you need a lawyer in the room. Business concerns are for you and your partner(s) to consider and decide. If you are inexperienced in these matters then you should consider the advice of consultants or professional advisors in this field.

7

WHEN IT'S "NOT" ABOUT MONEY...

When Forty Bucks Makes You a Millionaire

A friend of mine founded what is now the largest urban company in history, with revenues exceeding six billion dollars to date. His story is the perfect first example for this chapter.

He started the business in his garage in Queens. He had nothing but a few random pieces in his line. Though he had no experience owning a clothing company, he was holding on to the single most important factor, which would later lead to his tremendous dominance in the urban contemporary market, *hustle*.

A friend of his had achieved mega-stardom as a rap artist, known by the world over. He pleaded with his friend to wear one of his samples. Somewhat against his will, his friend granted his favor in order to get him off his back.

He used some more contacts to wardrobe some more recording artists and celebrities in the industry. He would take the few T-shirts he had, have the celebrities wear the shirts, then he would take them back, wash them and re-circulate them to more entertainers. As I said, he had *hustle*.

As his product became visible in the media, he closed a deal with one of the largest corporations in the world who became his strategic partner. He was the

ultimate marketer, and they had all the other pieces of the puzzle necessary to execute on the exposure he had created in the market.

His friend who did him the favor, later became extremely well compensated by him, and became a key spokesperson for the brand in the years to come.

His name is Daymond John, the company is FUBU, and his friend was the legendary rap artist, LL Cool J.

Did Daymond go after the money at first? Absolutely not. What he did do was create something that nobody else had and no investor in his or her right mind could ignore.

Why do I know all of this? Because the company that signed the deal with his company simultaneously dropped their deal with me when the demand for his product put them in the position where they couldn't afford to give us both the necessary attention... so I know the situation rather intimately. They actually gave us the opportunity to jump on board but we stubbornly refused, as we let our emotions and our egos cloud our judgment. (see #5)

Let's go a bit further...

If someone were to advertise their brand in a magazine during that time, it may cost thirty thousand dollars. If they wanted to run a thirty-second ad on television, it may cost them several hundred thousand dollars for one single exposure. So, what would it cost to run a ten-minute commercial on prime time television once a month for, say a year? If your math is at all good, it may cost well let's see.... Thirty seconds into ten minutes is twenty, multiplied times twelve times (for the year), multiplied times a few hundred thousand.... Pretty big number, huh? Almost fifty million dollars, give or take a few million.

Well, Daymond got the ten-minute commercial and more, as his product appeared quite a bit more than twelve times a year... and that is an understatement. FUBU was worn on prime-time television shows, music videos, cable stations like MTV and BET, you name it. Hundreds of hours of footage.

So what do you think it cost him? Fifty million? Perhaps forty million since they gave him a volume discount? Try about forty bucks. I say forty bucks as that was about the cost he paid to make a sweatshirt for a celebrity to wear on a show or a video. Most of the times it was a t-shirt or a hat so it cost even less. Remember, he was washing the few samples he had and re-circulating them, as he didn't have the money at first to make tons of samples. Not a bad price for exposing your product to hundreds of millions of people...but how can this be? And why forty bucks?

The answer to this question lies in a rather lucrative industry that became known as *product placement.* Product placement is an industry that became extremely controversial in our market. Protesters believed it gave free advertising to companies who didn't have the money to pay for it. Advocates thought it was a great way of leveling the playing field against the monstrous corporations that were unfairly dominating the market with their advertising dollars. I think it was just plain smart. Daymond John and FUBU was a big part of the revolution of product placement.

This first example is one of many huge parts of the deal that has absolutely zero to do with money. Well, not zero, but forty bucks... and that is not the only case where a small amount of money went a long way. Here's another thing that Daymond did…

Upon launching his collection, he figured New York was the best of all places to begin some local marketing. He went to all the top urban clubs in New York that would have the most concentrated amount of potential consumers and offered to make free jackets for the doormen and security to wear. He would add the club's logo in big bold letters on the back of the jackets and accompany the FUBU logo on the left chest and the sleeves. This was nothing but beneficial for the club for many reasons. First, many of the doormen were rather large and had a hard time finding anything in their size, and Daymond made sizes to fit everyone. Second, the staff now had a uniform which helped from a fashion standpoint to give the club further appeal, and functionally, the staff could be easily spotted in a crowd. Third, the club loved the idea of having their name on the jackets, and finally… it was all free!

To Daymond, while he was a hero to the club owners and staff, he was making out like a bandit himself as every hip kid in New York became exposed to the logo before his line ever hit the stores!

This small, strategic investment played a huge role in the initial success of the collection in New York, and he replicated the process in all the major metropolitan cities soon thereafter.

Free Equity

After about the first year or so in Entrig, we started selling additional shares of our company in attempts to generate more capital. Forty thousand dollars bought one investment share unit in the company (which represented roughly one percent of the company equity). Thus, if someone were to spend four hundred thousand dollars, they would receive a ten percent share in the company. I ended up giving two guys I knew a whopping forty-percent equity stake in the company. Did they pay the $1.6 million dollars that they were supposed to? Did I give them a break and settle on a million three? Any guesses?

I gave them the forty percent for a buck. One dollar. Was I ignorant? Did they hold a gun to my head? None of the above. Let me explain…

One of the guys, like in the previous example, was a celebrity, and the other one was an ex-basketball jock that knew every basketball player in the NBA. After two months time, our brand was known by the entire world over. We had placed Entrig product on over a hundred celebrities in both the sports and music arenas, and had appeared numerous times on prime time television. All in a few months.

Our logo was on every interview, concert, and photo shoot our celebrity partner attended. Since our celebrity partner was always acting in the best interests of the company, he took it even a step further and made sure any artist he appeared with was wearing the product as well. His group was even more famous overseas, so the exposure wasn't restricted to the United States alone, but worldwide. Sales came rushing in at a monster pace not only from the United States but also Japan, Germany, Korea, France and the UK.

This example is yet another one of the many cases where the deal isn't about money. When you put both sides on the scale, you would see that the advertising dollars we would have paid to get the same worldwide exposure that we received dwarfed the $1.6 million that we could have received if that 40% in equity had simply been sold to passive investors. Working smart once again demonstrates its advantage over working hard.

Sweat Equity

In my first company, I didn't have the money to afford any of the extensive legal work needed to protect my business from the onset. I had a real problem.

After speaking with many law firms practically begging for free legal work, I stumbled upon a concept I had never heard of that I would later find out was called *sweat equity*. After getting kicked out of practically every firm in town, I finally found a firm that truly seemed to believe in both my company and me as an individual. After telling them my concerns and financial restrictions, they seemed to still express interest in helping me. We came up with a deal between my company and their law firm. The deal was that we would give them a small piece of our company equity, in exchange for unlimited legal work (within reason, of course) in the future.

Know the difference between this example and case study #6. You are not getting anything for free and this has nothing to do with having a friend who is an attorney. This is an equity transaction. What you are agreeing *not* to pay now, you are agreeing to pay for later, provided that the company ever takes off.

This concept is called sweat equity. If someone believes in you, they will offer you such a deal. If not, it's a waste of their time. Their reward should you succeed however, will invariably be a lot higher than if you had paid them their regular fee from the onset.

Sweat equity can be a powerful inducement for many professionals to get involved early, especially if the services that they may perform are relatively pedestrian for them but critical for a young business to have performed. It is impossible for you to be an expert in every field that you will require a professional so if you find someone who is a professional showing interest in sweat equity, don't be shy about considering it and don't over play your hand by trying to scrimp on how much equity you allow. Remember, at the end of the day they are taking all of the risk and you are receiving all of the benefits, whether the company takes off or not.

Look at it this way… a $5,000 professional fee may as well be a $1 million professional fee if you've only got two dollars in your checking account. If you need the work to be done and you don't have the money, sweat equity may be the perfect option. Remember, nearly every startup has had to make sacrifices in order to get off the ground. Your equity will mean nothing if you never have the ability to get started.

Strategic Alliances

During the process of looking for new ideas for our upcoming advertising campaign, we contacted the director of marketing of one of the large record labels in the industry. They had recently signed a new artist and were launching his album around the same time that our new advertisement would hit the stands. After meetings back and forth, we devised a cooperative alliance between Entrig and the record label.

According to the terms of the agreement, we were obligated to use their artist in the ad campaign and put their logo and his album cover on our web site. The record label, in turn, was obligated to put our logo in their advertising campaign for the album release; require their street team to pass out Entrig postcards and T-shirts; and have our logo appear on their web site as well.

There were huge benefits for both sides, as both our company and theirs literally doubled both of our exposure in the market without spending an additional dollar in the marketing budget. Furthermore, they helped our exposure tremendously in areas where we were lacking exposure, and vice versa. For example, whereas our company was relatively new to the Internet and received only a few hundred hits a day, their web site was highly publicized and received several hundred thousand a day. On the other hand, we added significantly to the inherent value of their artist by signing him to an endorsement deal, which gave the consumer the perception that he was in high demand even before the release of his album. Finally, by collectively advertising in the same trade publications at the same time, we had two advertisements each month for the cost of one, as their ad showed our logo and our ad showed their artist.

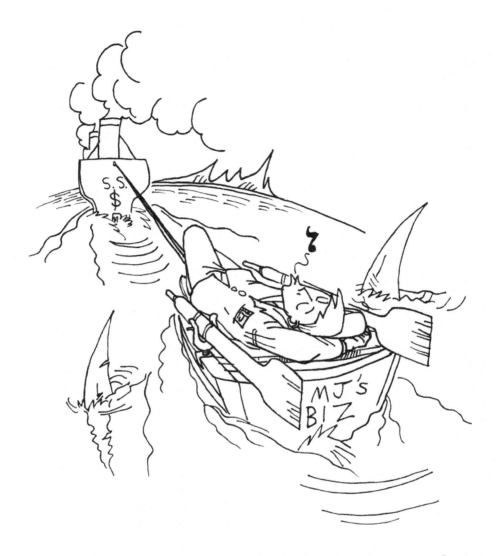

Under normal circumstances, we would have had to pay large sums of money to have their artist endorse our product. We knew, however, that the record label needed as much additional exposure of their new artist as possible, just as much as we needed an artist to appear in our advertisement. Since the relationship was nothing but mutually beneficial and added value to both parties, no money exchanged hands.

Performance Equity

As I mentioned earlier, our international business at Entrig seemed to be growing in popularity with our partner's group overseas.

We were contacted by a gentleman, Joe, who was interested in expanding our revenues even further in Europe, as he felt our brand had the potential of being one of the leading brands in the overseas market.

Though we were very interested in the prospect of increasing our business in Europe, we did not have the available funds to hire him exclusively to manage our European distribution. We already had distributors selling our product in Europe, but they were only customers, and we had no idea how our merchandise was being displayed and what the stores that carried our product looked like. Furthermore, there was huge counterfeiting in those countries and we had nobody representing our company to protect such things from happening.

We came up with a way that we could hire Joe full-time, while at the same time not costing us one penny out of pocket. Joe came to us telling us what he could do for the company and that, with his help, we could triple our business within one year. I decided to see if Joe was willing to put his money where his mouth was, and told him that I would pay him a percentage of any increase in revenues and/or new business generated. That way, for every additional dollar I made, I gave him a dime.

I succeeded in hiring someone full-time without having to pay him a salary. Do not confuse this with hiring someone for free, as I simply changed the compensation from salary to commission. The great thing about a commission-based compensation is that a person is rewarded on their performance only. They *"eat what they kill"* as the phrase goes. Just to clarify, I call it performance equity because it was a little more complicated than I explained above. The truth is that it was not just commission as we released a small amount of equity at certain milestones.

There are a few strong considerations when contemplating hiring someone on a commission, as I have explained in the previous chapters, so you need to weigh both the upside and the potential downside and decide what part of the scale outweighs the other. When you throw in a little equity I think it sweetens the pie a bit as the person then benefits from the company as a whole.

Brand Value

When our company was receiving the recognition I had always hoped, everyone was coming out of nowhere to solicit our business. There were the printers, the factories, the advertising agencies, the marketing firms, the magazines; you name it they showed up at our front door, especially the magazines. Every magazine in America came to us looking for advertising dollars, as we already were running ads heavily in the top four publications.

The problem for them, however, was that I knew how they worked; what they were thinking; and what type of deals they would accept from us because I had been in their position before. Let me explain...

When you have a clothing company, you want to get your brand into all the best stores. This is very hard to do, as there is a lot of competition out there and it is tough to be a part of the selection process for the top retailers unless you are already a proven company. So how do you get into the best store in the world (even though you may not deserve it)? Here's how....

When I wanted my brand to be in the best store out there, what did I do? I offered them my product...for free. Actually, not for free, but on consignment, which means they only pay what they can sell and then return anything that is remaining. That way, there was zero risk on the part of the retailer, as they weren't financially on the hook for one penny. If the product didn't sell, it was my loss not theirs. So why was this great for me?

After getting into the best store, I would go to the rest of the stores in the neighborhood and tell them I was in the best store up the street (I wasn't lying). When a retailer sees you are in the best stores in their neighborhood, you'd be surprised how quickly and suddenly they want your product. They feel that if that retailer bought your product, they should as well. Why? Because it is a heck of a lot harder to get into that retailer than theirs, so your line must be worthy of the sale.

This is how I knew the magazines would give me free advertisements, because by telling the other brands that I was advertising with them, they would significantly increase their chances of getting my competition to advertise with them as well. So I told the magazines I was not interested, knowing that they needed me even though they didn't want to admit it.

As expected, most would come back and offer to cut the cost in half. I still wouldn't bite because I knew I had something they needed ... *brand value*, something I had already created and they were attempting to achieve. Naturally, I was not going to pay them for something that was helping them more than me! Invariably, many of them gave me the ads for free. They then used that leverage to do to another company what I had just done to them. The end result if all goes well in these situations is that both companies always end up helping each other as the brand value of one brand will increase the brand value of another.

Here's how it did in this example...

If the magazine that *did not* give me the free ad went to my competitor, let's call them *"Company X"*, and showed them their magazine with my brand *not* in it, and Company X saw no other familiar brands advertising in the publication, they would feel no need to advertise either.... If, on the other hand, after getting my ad in their publication, Company X saw my advertisement, that would both lend instant credibility to the publication and give Company X an incentive to advertise so that my company didn't get an unfair advantage.

No one ever has to know that I didn't pay for the ad and, of course, the magazines made me promise I would never divulge this to anyone, in the same way I asked the retailer not to tell anyone my merchandise was on consignment. That's the beauty of it, and how many businesses in general get started.

Let me drill this concept in your head with one final point. Let's say I walk into a crowded bar and attempt to make conversation with some women at the bar. They may or may not give me the time of the day. If, however, I walk in with Lebron James and try to do the same thing, what happens then? Of course, all of a sudden, every girl and their mother want to be my best friend. Is it because of me? Of course not, I'm simply in the company of someone who suddenly increases the value of how other people feel about me. The same holds true when you represent a magazine and you are in good company (your advertisers are well known)... suddenly everyone wants to be in your next issue.

8

WHEN TRUST IS A FOUR-LETTER WORD ...

In this chapter, I have taken a different approach from the previous chapters. Remember back in the introduction when I told you the story about the son, the father, and the snake? You will also remember that I told you that I am an expert at the art of avoiding snakes and how to steer clear from them and/or eliminate them when they get in your path.

Well, you have now been witness to my stories and, hopefully can use each and every one of them to your utmost advantage. What would happen however, if in a few months after reading this book you forgot most of the information, never took my advice to keep a copy of this book in your hip pocket (or phone), and you ran into a snake? That's the purpose of this chapter...

Unfortunately, only a small percent of people read through more than a few chapters of any given book, and those that do happen to read the book cover to cover, don't typically go back to it and actually apply the lessons they learned. It is a fact that memory retention after reading a book only lasts for a little while and you forget most of what you read unless you continuously go back to it.

In case such a thing happens to you, in this chapter I am attempting to summarize the most important lessons gained from this book, briefly and to the point (I guess you can say I'm giving you the *cliff notes* from the preceding chapters).

It takes all the war stories, all the tragedies, and all the lessons learned, and it picks out the common threads that seem to tie all these mistakes together. I then break them down (even repeating myself at times) in attempts to pound them into your head one last time before you're out on your own in the forest.

If you took the time to review all of the case studies in detail up to this point, you will notice there are a few common strings that tie them all together. What are they? Think about it. OK I'll help you...

Trust

I am going to say a few things about trust in this section that may come across a bit callous and paranoid so let me clarify a few things before I move on...

Trust is one of the greatest gifts in both life and business, and running your own business with people you can trust is one of the most enjoyable and fulfilling experiences of an entrepreneur's journey. Trust, however, cannot be given freely, as it *must be earned*. You may have noticed that nearly all of the case studies I document in this book where I had problems with trust came from experiences that happened when I entered a new relationship, not an old one where trust had already been established. Please make sure you are clear on this.

Entrepreneurs put everything they have into their businesses. Because of this, it is insane to let someone simply come in and destroy what has taken you so much blood, sweat and tears to build. There simply is no logic in trusting someone you have just met or have no relationship with.

I think of trust in business very much like locking your doors at night before you go to sleep. To me, my business is my home and I need to protect my house at all times so nobody hurts me… or my family. For this reason, I have learned to lock my doors when I need to.

To most intruders, a locked door is a deterrent and the potential intruder will move on to the next house on the block that maybe left their screen door open. If someone knocks on my door, I look through the peephole to see who it is. If it is a stranger, I may open the door but keep the chain on the lock and ask them what they want. You must protect your business like you protect your house and follow these same rules. Remember, trust is earned, not given.

Trust is by far the biggest and most common fault made throughout my journey as an entrepreneur. In the previous chapters you should have noticed that I went into business with my doors unlocked and reaching for every snake and getting bitten nearly every time. I *trusted* a factory to do my production when they didn't even have the equipment. I *trusted* the sales organization that stole my commissions. I *trusted* that the salesperson at the printing factory had credited my account. I *trusted* both the mill and the factory that stole my merchandise and tried to sell it back to me for double. I *trusted* the distributor who gave me an order for seven million dollars. I *trusted* the investor who agreed to give me four hundred thousand dollars. I *trusted* the investor who was giving me a million-dollar bank check. I trusted, I trusted, I trusted… and lost two businesses and the shirt off my back as a result.

When I entered business for the first time, my father gave me one piece of advice, and told me the rest I would have to figure out for myself. He said, "*Ninety-nine percent of all the people you will meet in business are full of shit…*"

When he told me this I was furious. I was so excited to go into business, build relationships and become successful that I felt he was spoiling the entire enjoyment of the process. Because of this, I chose to completely ignore him and go by the philosophy that everyone I came into contact with was innocent until proven guilty.

As it turned out, *I should've listened to my father.*

If you are reading this book and looking forward to starting a new business, this may bring you down in the same way my father brought me down many years ago but it shouldn't at all and that is not my intention. It is all about what I mentioned a few paragraphs ago… protecting your house. For instance, I have a current partner who loves to remind me that he has made much more money working with people he never trusted than he has ever made with friends and family. How could this be possible? He knew what he was dealing with and he kept his "house" locked down under very tight security.

In business, being an *optimist* is optional, but being a *realist* is required. The *real* is that my father was right and that comment has proved to be the rule rather than the exception throughout my entire business career, as I trusted people who I had no business trusting in the first place. So as it relates to trusting people you do not know or are meeting for the first time, my recommendation would be as follows:

> *Trust no one.*
> *Expect nothing.*
> *Have no false hopes and no false expectations.*
> *Take verbal promises with a grain of salt.*
> *Pay special attention to the ones that promise you the world.*
> *Remember the talkers never walk, and the walkers never talk.*
> And, most importantly…
> *Put everyone's money where their mouths are and get it on paper. Dot every "i";*
> *cross every "t"; wait till the ink is dry; go over your checklist five times…and don't*
> *trust a soul until they earn your trust!*

Sounds pretty paranoid, doesn't it? Before, you answer, go back to the example of the house. Ask yourself if you would you leave your doors unlocked for people to enter who you don't know or are meeting for the first time. Apply that logic to your business and you should be fine. Like Under Armour says, *Protect This House!*

One final point on trust…

Have you noticed how the infamous *never go on a suicide mission* example (#18) seemed to recur in nearly every story in the later chapters? Did you ever think why? Well, again, it's the issue of trust. Every investor seemed to promise the money at some point, and no one ever seemed to come through in the end. And what did I do when I heard we were getting the money? I stopped everything else I was doing and cleared everything off my plate as if the deal was signed and the money was in the bank. How differently things would have turned out had I gone in then with the information I know now.

Trust but verify. Let's move on…

Honesty and Kindness

There were a few other recurring faults made in the horror stories of this book that are important to look at.

Honesty in many cases is a mistake. I know it sounds horrible to say, but it's true, nonetheless. Why is this? Put simply, honesty that falls on the wrong ears exposes weakness.

Does this mean you should lie? Not at all. It means that, before opening your mouth, you should always think it through three times about what you say and to whom you say it to. The less a competitor knows about your future plans, the stronger you become when your plan is executed. I know it's pretty stupid to think anyone would tell a competitor or enemy privileged information, however you'd be absolutely amazed how information travels and winds up in the ears of the unintended.

Do you remember back in high school when you told your best friend your best kept secret and made him or her promise not to tell anyone? What happened? If your high school experience was like mine, somehow, some way, everyone in the school knew that secret by the end of the week…and what did you do? Naturally, you asked your best friend if they had said anything, and of course, they denied it and promised they hadn't said a word. The only problem was that they were the only person you told, so naturally, they were lying to you. How horrible is that? Your best friend telling your deepest, darkest secret!

Right then and there, you received your first lesson on trust. If you can't even trust the ones closest to you, how do you expect to trust anyone else? Here's one of my father's favorite quotes from his favorite movie, *The Godfather* … *"Keep your friends close and your enemies closer."* I wish he had told me that back in junior high.

Remember how nice I was to my new employee, Jon back in Chapter Five (#27)? What happened? He ended up walking all over me. So what's the answer?

Do you have to be a scrooge in order to be a successful entrepreneur? Of course not. Here are some rules to go by when it comes to honesty and kindness…

When you hire someone, while I believe honesty and kindness is of paramount importance, I believe that can only work if both parties have mutual respect for one another. If there is mutual respect between employer and employee (I hate those words as I hate titles in general), the honesty and kindness is not mistaken for weakness and the relationship is on solid ground. When honesty and kindness is mistaken for weakness (as is often the case), all hell breaks loose. Personal calls, personal emails, disregard for authority, dissension between peers, sick days, buffered expense accounts, long lunches, late arrivals, early departure, I've seen it all.

I think it is very important to explain the lay of the land in the beginning. Telling people what is expected and what is not expected gives them the information they need so that if they do something wrong, they know they are doing it wrong because they were told in the beginning. If they do something wrong *and they know it,* I believe it should be brought to their attention with no consequence the first time unless it is scandalous to the point that you have no choice. If it happens again, make sure you back up what you said you were going to do. You have to be willing to walk your talk, or the talk was worthless.

Let me give you an example that came way before my life as a businessman... When I was growing up, whenever I would get into trouble, my dad would tell me the next time I screwed up I would be grounded. When the next time would come, he would tell me he was giving me one last chance to clean up my act... and then one more, and one more, etc., etc. Naturally, I never stopped my bad ways because I never got grounded. At first, it seemed he meant business, but when I realized he didn't carry through on his threats, I walked all over the rules of the house as if they never existed. That is why you must do what you say. You cannot be afraid to let a person go who is blatantly refusing to play by the rules. It's not like you didn't tell him (or her) the rules in the beginning.

Another big problem in the business world is the things that take place the moment you walk out the door. I'm sure you've heard the saying, *"when the cat's away, the mice will play."* You will see in the upcoming chapters some examples of what happened when I left my office without regard to the mice.

Emotion

Emotion, on the other hand, regardless of whether it's positive or negative, gets you into trouble more times than not. If you get too excited about something (positive emotion), you expose yourself and lose your poker face, and all successful entrepreneurs are required to play a great game of poker. Furthermore, it can distract and confuse you into doing something you would have never done had you taken the emotion away from the situation, as in the case of giving my only samples to the celebrity and leaving myself empty-handed for a huge presentation (case study #4).

Getting excited in a bad way on the other hand, leads to quick and hasty decisions which are quite often, severely detrimental to your business. Such was a case when I got into the ugly shouting match with my finance company (case study #3). Furthermore, getting overly excited before the ink is dry on a deal leads to countless let downs and disappointments, which can eventually lead to health problems. As you read of all the deals of mine that never came to fruition (#'s 40-49), I was excited and nearly jumping for joy at some point along the way in each and every story.

The disappointment you feel when the deal falls apart can be devastating. Furthermore, going from such a high point to such a low point can be seriously detrimental to your health. In my case, that emotional roller coaster broke me down both physically and mentally, put me in the emergency room, and nearly left me close to losing it altogether.

Remember that if you don't control your emotions, your emotions will control you.

9

TRICKS OF
THE TRADE ...

In this chapter, you will learn some valuable tricks and habits that will both help you profit from your business and protect you from snooping predators looking to steal what you have worked so hard to acquire. You'd be amazed how seemingly harmless habits can leave your business exposed to huge potential problems.

Section One... When Technology Sucks

For most businesses, the information in your computer contains both your most important documents and your most sensitive. As we live in a society where technological advances have made such things as a pencil and paper nearly extinct and has turned huge day planners and address books into apps on your smart phone, these advances have, in most cases, helped our society work more efficiently from both the standpoint of time and convenience. In fact, the times of men carrying large briefcases filled with documents, seems to have been replaced by technologies that can store all the information, previously in a briefcase, into a gadget that fits in the palm of your hand or in your breast pocket.

On the other side of the coin, for many, this technology has made us lazy and overly dependent. In fact, the creation of such technology has often led to absolute devastation. Let me tell you about a few of mine...

50 Why This Book Almost Never Existed

The Wrong:

When writing this book, I didn't really do any editing until the book was completed because I had so much information running around in my brain I had to get it all on paper as quickly as possible. Often times, I would write for eight or nine hours at a time without getting out of my chair because I was afraid I would lose my train of thought. You should also know that writing this book was both painful and cathartic at the same time, since I had to relive every bad experience and mistake I had ever made in business, and then analyze and break the experience down for you. I would often find myself shaking my head while I wrote, as I couldn't believe half the mistakes I had made.

Chapter Three of this book happened very quickly as I pumped out the chapter in about five or six hours. After finishing, it was after dark, so I figured I'd save the file to a disk and get some *br-unch-inner* (the word I use for breakfast, lunch and dinner when I only have time to eat one meal per day) before starting the next chapter.

Halfway through saving the file to disk (yes there were floppy's back then), something strange happened and the computer froze. I couldn't move the cursor, and there was no way to know how much information had been saved if any. I sat looking at the screen for hours trying to figure out what to do. I hadn't taken the time to save any of the work along the way, since I had been so immersed in the writing, so I knew there was a chance I would lose all the information. Finally, I decided there was nothing I could do but restart the computer and pray most of the information was saved.

Needless to say it was not. I lost everything. I was so angered and frustrated I literally almost threw the computer out the window. I told myself, *f!ck* it and decided in a moment of rage, to give up writing the book. It wasn't so much the time I had put in, but the passion I had poured out that couldn't be replaced.

When you say or write something for the first time, I feel it is always by far your best work. I felt that there was no chance I could muster up the energy to start over with the same details, wit and enthusiasm. So, there I sat, eyes burning, neck stiff, shoulders sore, and hungry as hell since I hadn't eaten. I felt like I had just lost a family member.

I figured the only thing I could do was call that friend, you know, the friend that everyone has, that is commonsensical and level headed about every situation, that you feel like strangling him... So I told him what happened. I spilled out all of the rage and anger and frustration. He didn't say a word until I had spit it all out. Then he responded…

He told me to replace everything. Replace the hunger by eating. Replace the burning eyes by taking a nap. Replace my stiff neck by taking a hot shower, and replacing my sore shoulders by getting a massage…and not to even think about going back to the computer until the next day. He knew that I was a complete morning person and that there is nothing I feel I cannot do early in the morning with a cup of hot coffee in hands. I also knew it was now late and dark, my absolute worst time of the day to do any work, so I knew his advice to start the next day with a fresh head was sound advice. I did this and began the chapter again the following morning. I'm not going to lie, it was extremely aggravating at first, but I got through it...and haven't looked back since. In fact, I think the chapter I rewrote is better than the original.

What was the lesson learned? Save! Save! Save! From that point forward, you can only imagine how often I saved my work.

The Right:

Here are the most important things to remember to avoid any such problems:

First, if you are going to buy a computer, most computers now have an **AutoSave** function, which saves your work automatically after a certain time period. If you are buying one or you own one, check and see if your computer has this function. If it does, check if you can modify the frequency, as well. For example, thirty minutes is way too long between save times for me, as some of my information is too valuable to risk even ten minutes of information. If you can, set the AutoSave every five or ten minutes.

Second, even if you have AutoSave, **manually save** your work every time you finish a page, or every five to ten minutes, whichever comes sooner. Though it may seem a bit tiresome and redundant, it can save you from a world of heartache, believe me.

It is also important to remember that hard drives crash out of the blue many times for no apparent reason...probably just to keep you on your toes. Because of this, it is important to **save your file to an external hard drive and the cloud** every time you save it to your hard drive. I use *Drop box* and *Google Drive*. Though this may take an additional thirty seconds or so, should anything happen with your hard drive, you are now protected externally and in the cloud as well.

Additionally, after saving to your hard drive, external drive and the cloud, if it is an indispensable document (like a book) **print out a hard copy**. Should your computer have a virus, it may corrupt both your hard drive as well as your external drive, and I don't trust the cloud 100% either. Even if you have two hundred pages printed, don't worry, because at the very worst, you can go to any number of a million word processing locations and have a professional typist retype it in a matter of a few hours for a fairly reasonable price.

Which brings me to the next point... get **anti-virus software** and run it on both your hard drive and external drives every time before you start your work. Macs don't have many issues with viruses at this point, which is one of the main reasons why I use a Mac.

The final step you may think is paranoid, but believe me, it has happened to more people than you can count. Suppose you have followed all the steps. You have saved everything to your hard drive, you have saved everything to a disk... and you have printed everything out. Are you completely covered? Absolutely not. Here's another story which, for the first time I can say, did *not* happen to me but to someone I know....

I had a girlfriend that followed all these steps and she followed them meticulously and without fail. She was a graphic artist who lived in a basement apartment in Manhattan and backed up all of her work by all the ways I outlined above (except the cloud because that option hadn't been created yet).

She had her portfolio on her computer, on disk, and kept a full hard copy of her originals in the apartment as well. One day, after a huge rainstorm, she came home to find out the outside drain to the porch was clogged and her entire apartment was flooded. Everything was ruined. Everything. Ten years of work was destroyed by water. She was absolutely devastated.

The final two steps to saving your work should leave you as close to complete protection as possible. The first step in the final phase is to **e-mail yourself** your work every time before you leave your home or office. That way, if God-forbid something should happen to your apartment, whether it is a flood, fire, theft, or any other natural disaster, you are protected. If it is a word-processing document like this one, it'll only take a second or two even if it's a few hundred pages in length. If it's graphics, however, it may take a minute or two, but it's worth it.

Finally, take a full set of your work, both hard copy and disk, and **give a copy to a family member or friend** to hold onto. That way, both your place and theirs would have to burn down the same day to lose your information.

#51 How I lost Touch With Three Hundred of My Closest Friends

The Wrong:

The same holds true for all new technology in general. When I got my first palm pilot (yes palm pilot), I thought it was the coolest thing in the world. I took nearly

twenty pages of phone numbers and put all the information in the palm pilot on a six-hour flight from New York to Las Vegas. When I got to Vegas, I threw out all the scrap pieces of paper that had previously held all the names and numbers, and was happy that all the information I needed was now at my fingertips.

As you can probably guess, a few months later, I dropped my palm pilot and broke it. I had no back up of the names, addresses and phone numbers because I had been too lazy to back it up on my hard drive. To this day, there are still several hundred people I cannot contact because I failed to save my information in more than one place. I guess, in a way, this is another living example of the downfalls of going on a suicide mission.

The same holds true for **smart phones.** As you are probably aware, smart phones have the capacity to store thousands of names and numbers as well. When I received such a phone for the first time, I saved all the numbers on the phone, so I could access hundreds of people at the touch of a button. One day, I dropped my phone and it broke. As you can imagine, I had none of the numbers stored in any other place, as I had thrown out the hard copies upon entering all the numbers into my phone.

To show you how horrible technology can be, I had to wait for my three closest friends to call me. I had no idea what their phone numbers were, because they had always been associated with a speed-dial number in my phone directory. When I told my best friend that I didn't even know his phone number, instead of being angry, he admitted he hadn't a clue what mine was either.

The Right:
Today, **smart phones can be synced** with your computer or even your email quite easily. All that is required is a simple extra step. On my phone for example, every time I save a number I merge it with my backup Google mail and it saves the contact. That way, if anything happens I still have all of the information saved.

I would still, however, save your most important information on disk and in print, and in two or more places.

Section 2... *When the Door to Your Office Is Always Open... Without You in It*

#52 How I Made My Deepest Secrets Public Knowledge

The Wrong:
I kept a legal file in my office that contained all the originals of the contracts that were signed between my company and anyone we were under contract with.

When the president of our finance company claimed I had defaulted on a loan, I immediately went to the vice-president who I had paid the loan back to a few months before. He told me he had used the money for himself and begged me not to tell the president. When I refused, he told me that he would deny it and, since I had written the check to cash, I could not trace who the person was who deposited the check. Luckily, I had made him sign a receipt when I paid the loan back, and had it in my legal file.

When I went to find the signed receipt, somehow, it was missing from my legal file. Since that was the only place I had ever put such documents, I knew that it could be in no other place, and I suspected foul play.

Furthermore, when a sales group that refused to pay me commissions claimed they were never informed such an arrangement was made between their group and ours, I immediately went to the legal file, as I had them sign a contract when the agreement took place. When I went to retrieve the agreement…it was missing as well.

As it turned out, I would later find out that my private office was like a revolving door after hours, as people would go into my files, look through my check registers, you name it, they did it. All my private information was public after hours and my office went from door closed, lights off, computer shut-down, to almost as if there was a second shift who came in to use my office from sunset to sunrise. When I learned of this, I felt thoroughly invaded.

There wasn't a whole lot I could do as my office was inside the office of my financing company, so there were always other people around at all hours, especially since it was a Chinese company and most of their calls were made late at night because of the time difference with the factories overseas.

The Right:

Every person in my office knew where my legal file was, as it was bright yellow and in the drawer under my desk. I just never thought anyone would ever go into my personal space and steal what was rightfully mine. I guess you can say, I *trusted* no one would do such a thing.

First and foremost, always make copies of any important documents and take them home with you. That's a must.

Second, buy a safe for your office and put all of your sensitive information in the safe…and make sure you know what is sensitive and what is not. For example, there may be many things in your office, which you take for granted, which many people would die to get, like your customer list or client profiles, for example. Also, always include check registers, financial statements, sales reports, and any and all future designs and ideas. *Do not get this confused with a drawer with a lock on it.* Such drawers can be opened a million different ways with a butter knife. Trust me, I know as I've opened locked drawers may times when I didn't bring or couldn't find my key.

#53 How to Become Your Competitor's #1 Employee ...Without Knowing It

The Wrong:

Each season, the strengths of our company lay in our ability to create innovative and unique strategies, both in design and marketing. Since our showroom was connected to the offices of our finance company, there were constantly clients and competitors in our office, and we had to be careful about what was lying around or in open view. As it turned out, we needed to be a bit more careful than just that.

Both the art computer and my personal computer had all the future designs and layouts we had planned for the upcoming seasons. Every night before I left, I would shut off the computer and close my door just to make sure no one would snoop around looking to copy my ideas.

As a few seasons went by, I would consistently notice that some of our designs and advertising ideas would spring up from our competitors. I suspected it was beyond coincidence, as many of these ideas were way too far out there for our competitors to think of.

One day, I saw a business prospectus of a competitor of ours lying on the desk of the president of the sales organization that had stolen our commissions. I actually thought it was our old plan so I picked it up and read the first page, and then the second, then the third. It was nearly verbatim of our company business prospectus (only replaced by another company's name). This was tremendously upsetting to Gary and I as it had taken us a very long time complete. Sixty plus pages on market conditions, financial projections, management requirements, selling tactics, public relations plans, you name it... I remember thinking, *how the hell did he get an entire copy of my business prospectus?*

As it turns out, it came from me... more specifically, my computer.

The Right:

First and most importantly, set a password for your computer so that only you can enter your hard drive after you shut it down... and don't tell a soul what the password is.

Second, set another password for your screensaver and set your screensaver to thirty seconds, no matter how many times you have to type in your password throughout the day.

As it turned out, he had stolen my customer list as well, and sold both the prospectus and customer list to my competitor. I knew this because I checked when the files were last opened and noticed they were both opened after I had left the office.

I'm glad I could be of assistance to my competitor (despite the fact that I never received a thank-you note).

#54 How to Guarantee You Won't Get the Order

The Wrong:

When I started my first business, I immediately had order forms printed up for when I wrote business. I noticed that it was very difficult writing up new business, however my sales representative in Philadelphia was turning in orders hand over fist. So much so, I was glad he had his own order forms, as I would have run out of money getting them printed if he had used mine.

One day, after hiring a new sales rep, I sent her a bunch of order forms, as she wanted to use our company letterhead when writing her orders. When she received the order forms, she sent them right back. I thought it was a mistake, so I called her to tell her I was resending the forms for the next day's delivery, as they had been returned to our office by accident.

She called me back and told me she decided not to represent us. I was shocked, as she had been so excited to represent us. When I asked her what the problem was, she said, *"I thought you told me you were doing a lot of business? Why did you lie to me?"* I told her I wasn't lying, and that we were doing the business that I had said. She responded, *"So how come you sent me order forms that start with #0001?"*

The Right:

Dumped over an order form? Seems pretty trivial, huh? Not at all.

No one ever wants to be the laboratory rat. The sales rep thought we hadn't written an order because we sent her order forms beginning with #0001, which eludes to the fact that there had never been an order up until that point. The truth was, our rep in Philadelphia had his own order forms that already were in the thousand range which showed a lot of business had been written up until that point and, believe me, that means a lot to a customer.

When getting order forms printed, or tickets, or anything where quantity means something, start with a high number that is not a multiple of 100, like 2,371. That way, you don't give anyone a further excuse not to order… and printing up order sheets beginning with "0001" is a sure way to guarantee you never get the order.

#55 How to Spend Ten Years Losing Money

The Wrong:
After both the first business and the second, millions of dollars had run through my company bank account. Each and every season, hundreds of thousands of dollars were being paid out to our creditors, more inventory and equipment were bought, and every penny we had left over was consistently being reinvested into the company.

As the company went through its peaks and valleys, my focus stayed steady and strong to continue feeding the profits and growing the company bigger and stronger in hopes to one day sell it and live off the profits.

When it was all said and done, and both businesses were over, I didn't have a pot to piss in or a window to throw it out of.

The Right:
Make money on every check.

A friend of mine went on a suicide mission. He represented a very large retailer in the United States and made one single item with them, season after season and year after year. He built a very large business as he made nearly eight million sweatshirts a year for the company, until one day, they stopped doing business with him and picked a competitor who could make it for a nickel cheaper.

When I learned of this, I went to visit him to tell him I heard the news and that I was sorry to hear they had taken the business away from him.

He responded, *"Thanks, but it's probably better off. I wanted to retire anyway."* I asked him if he was serious about retiring, as I didn't think he had the money to retire at his young age.

"I planned for this," he said, *"That's why I put aside a quarter for every sweatshirt I made, in case of a rainy day."* In three and a half years, he had made over twenty-four million sweatshirts for them. Multiply that times twenty-five cents a garment and do the math. As a matter of fact, I think he had enough for his kids to retire as well.

… And what a fun rainy day I am guessing he is still having.

10

DOING MATH WITH THE WRONG CALCULATOR

One of the things I became particularly fond of during the course of running both businesses was the number crunching. Projected revenues, anticipated profits, general and administrative expenses, marketing budgets, etc. Though this is an area that most creative entrepreneurs despise, I loved it and happened to be pretty good at it as well... or so I thought.

Like many other areas of the business, number crunching was something that I had to do to see if I could pad our margins a bit. Because I have never been averse to being self-taught, I dove into numbers with vigor from the onset. I went to the library, read up on all the public financial records of all the fashion companies on file, and collected dozens of financial reports of privately owned businesses as well, until I was able to understand the recurring formulas, percentages, and other numbers that all the companies seemed to share in common. I also learned the importance of making distinctions between marketing driven companies like ours who required a huge portion of our overall budget for advertising, compared to commodity-driven companies who focused mainly on price. When it was all said and done, I was extremely confident in running our company numbers from that point forward.

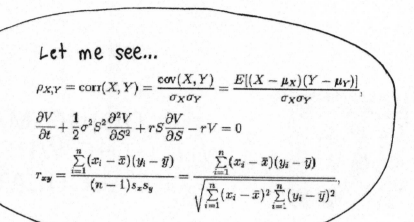

The problem however, was that after all the literature I had read on every competitive company in the market, I noticed that, at the end of the day, something was missing. Something had been left out. Maybe something hadn't been added or subtracted, or maybe multiplied or divided, but whatever it was, the numbers never added up in the end. Somehow my numbers seemed to be different from the others. There was still some calculation missing that I was overlooking.

I later realized exactly what that missing calculation was. The problem, however, is that this calculation is missing from every calculator in the world and, in order to get the right number at the end of the day, you have to use your own, custom calculator to get the number correct. Let me explain...

Picture a calculator. All calculators are pretty much the same though some have options that even accountants never use. But let's just think of a regular fifth grade calculator. Zero through nine, addition, subtraction, multiplication and division.

In business, there is one button that is missing that you have to always take into account or you will always find your company's finances gasping for air... It's called, *The Murphy Button*. What is the Murphy button? First, let me give you a brief overview on *MJ Accounting 101* so you gain a quick knowledge on how a business's numbers work as they all work basically the same.

"MJ Accounting 101"

When you begin your company, no matter what business you are in, you will need to devise something called a **projected income statement**. This will show yourself, your partner(s) and your investors how you plan to actually make money from what you are doing, how much you plan to make, and how long it will take to make it. It will show how you will spend your money, how much you will save, how much you will reinvest... basically it shows everything. Remember, anyone can start a business, but very few can make a penny in the process.

In the most simplistic terms, the formula is as follows:

Sales - Cost of Sales = Gross Profit.

This is the first and most important thing to know, however I'm guessing you may know this already. The problem however, is that most people don't interpret the cost of sales correctly. This was always my problem. So let's break it down in detail. Take a look at the following example...

Suppose you want to start a business that sells T-shirts. What is step one? What do you do? Do you just print up some shirts and go to a store hoping to get the sale? Of course it is not that simple. Believe it or not, this is the exact point where most businesses fail, as most businesses fail before the bell to round one even starts. So let's look into the steps to be taken to prevent this from happening.

First and foremost, when you start a business, **research** the market you want to be in up and down, side to side, and with a fine-tooth comb. Know what you are getting into and make sure you are comfortable with the demands before you take the jump. I can tell you that many entrepreneurs, if they *really* knew what they were getting into from the start, would have never gone into business in the first place. So do your research before stepping into the ring.

You must also know that most research is free (if you know how to get it) so you can gather as much information as you want to come to the right decision, and it won't cost you anything but time. There is nothing you cannot find out, when you combine the resources of the Internet and the public library. Me personally, I did not stop there. I went to university libraries that specialized in my field, as there are always certain times of the week when these libraries are open to the public. Furthermore, a great place to go is Barnes and Noble, as they encourage you to come in and read whatever they have on their shelves inside the store. So much so that they put chairs and couches all over their stores to encourage people to do just that.

So now, you've done your research on the industry and have decided you want to move forward. What is the next step? I'm sure you've heard before that if you want to be or do something, the best place to start is to **pick a role model** that is who you want to be or is doing what you want to be doing. You then simply find out what they did to get to where they are... and do the same thing. Well, it's not as simple as that but it does put you in an infinitely greater position to succeed.

As crazy as it may seem, this seemingly simple advice packs a ton of punch. No sense in re-inventing the wheel when someone else has paved a clear path. The same rule applies in the business world. In fact, one of my business partners, who is an accomplished martial artist, is always spouting bits of wisdom his martial arts master taught him from early adolescence well into adulthood. One of the truisms he likes to repeat is, *"Master Lee would tell me to live my life using a map written by someone who has been successful... If no such map exists then it is better to use a map written by a man who has failed rather then to go through life with no map at all."*

So what is step three? **Identify a competitor** in your market who has already succeeded and figure out how they made it. Of course, the tricky thing is that no competitors in their right mind will tell you how they succeeded, as they have enough competition as is, so you simply have to work backwards.

Let's look at the following example...

Working Backwards

You start by going into a store and find your competitor's brand. Let's call them, *Brand X* and let's call the store, *MJ's*. Let's say they are a clothing brand and you are most interested in T-Shirts because that is the category where you will be competing with them the most. This is where you start your initial back-to-front investigation. Your mission now is to use *Brand X* and **run the numbers**. First, write down the retail cost of that shirt. Now you know the price you ultimately want the consumer to pay for your T-shirt, but remember, you will be selling to the store, not the consumer, so your journey does not end there.

Next, you need to know what *Brand X* sold the shirt to *MJ's* for. Hopefully, from all the research you have done up until this point, you know what a typical retailer markup is on such a product (markup is the difference between what the store paid for the product and what the store is charging the customer). If you don't know the markup don't sweat it. There is no time like the present to learn how to figure that one out. Remember, one of the biggest parts of business is coming up with solutions to unanswered questions. The solutions are always there, you just need to know how to get them. Let me help a little…

There are a million ways to find out this type of information. One way is to go to the websites of all the brands in your market, as many of them have the contact information of their sales representatives on their site. The sales representatives are the people who sell to the store. Next, you will have to do a little creative talking and speak to the sales representative as if you were the buyer or owner of the store. I have found the best way to do this is to tell them you will be opening up a store. This way, they have to take your word for it because they have no store to call. In other words, do whatever you have to do (within the law) to find out the necessary information to *run the numbers*. Remember, this example has nothing to do with the fashion industry but to business in general. It is all about collecting information.

A good way to look at it is from the movie *Wall Street*. Remember when Charlie Sheen illegally poked around the office for information to get for Gordon Gekko? That was illegal and wrong. This is the legal and smart version of doing your homework and gathering good intelligence on your industry. In our industry, if *MJ's* is selling the shirt for twenty dollars, *Brand X* probably charged them about ten dollars, but that differs in every market, so it is your responsibility to do your homework in that department before your investor asks you.

So now you know what *Brand X* charged *MJ's*. To make things a bit trickier, let's throw another retail store in the mix. Let's call the store, *Gary's*. Let's say that both *Gary's* and *MJ's* paid the same price for *Brand X*. Does that mean they both sell it to the consumer for the same price? Not necessarily and there are some very justifiable reasons why. *MJ's* may reside in a more expensive neighborhood than *Gary's* and must charge higher prices to both keep up with the upscale reputation of the store so they are not perceived as cheap in that area. Another reason may be because they need to make more margin on each piece because they pay a much higher rent and *Gary's* is in a much more affordable area.

Another reason may be, where *Gary's* bought twelve shirts for ten dollars, *MJ's* may have bought twelve hundred shirts for eight dollars, and have received a volume discount from Brand X.

OK, let's take *Gary's* out of the mix and get back to *your brand, Brand X* and *MJ's*...

So now that you know what *MJ's* is selling *Brand X* for, and what *Brand X* is selling their shirts to *MJ's* for, you have a pretty good sense of what you will sell your shirts for, right? Not necessarily... In order to sell the shirt for the same price as *Brand X*, you need to look at the brand value of *Brand X*. You need to look at how much exposure in the market *Brand X* has created; how *Brand X* markets their product; how much they advertise; if there are any special qualities in the shirts that make them more valuable; and other things of the sort.

If, after analyzing these factors, you believe everything about your brand and *Brand X* are the same, then selling the product for the same price is probably a smart move. Right? Sounds right, but remember one crucial thing... you are not *Brand X*, at least not yet. This is the next thing you need to know. Always know your market position. It is just as important to **know where you are**, as it is to know where you want to be.

Don't expect to be treated the way *Brand X* is treated or you're in for an awfully big surprise. You may have the same quality product, be willing to spend the same amount of advertising dollars and create as much exposure in the market, but the simple truth is that you still don't know whether or not your product will sell because you have no track record. *Brand X* has a history with *MJ's*... you don't. It is important to get this so you understand *MJ's* perspective and the reason why they value you differently. I can't explain to you enough how important it is to know what is going on inside the mind of the person sitting on the other side of the table. You need to earn your respect from the retailer, you can't just expect it because your product looks and feels the same... or even if it looks and feels better.

Let's take things a bit further...

So let's suppose you plan to sell *MJ's* your shirt for the same ten dollars that *Brand X* charges. You make the shirt, analyze the cost down to the half penny, and realize that there is no way you can sell the shirt for ten dollars, because it is costing you eleven dollars! How can this be?

The answer again is volume. When you start in business, no matter what business, the more you buy, the cheaper everything becomes. What may be costing you eleven dollars may cost *Brand X* four dollars because you are making two hundred t-shirts and they are making twenty thousand. Does the retailer care what your costs are? Of course not.

Know that it takes money to make money, and that you must be willing to **make concessions** in the beginning and put your money where your mouth is until your market position becomes important. Free goods, discounts, allowances, concessions, whatever you choose to call it, you need to budget it. This of course was not in *Brand X's* financial reports, so how were you supposed to know? Bottom line is, a start-up company works off an entirely different formula, as I'm sure you are now beginning to realize.

Note: Truth is, it probably was in Brand X's report but you need to know where to look for it. It is normally under what they call 'dilution' or 'allowance for bad debt' however income statements are creative for a reason (to look good) so a lot of this information is often hidden in other areas.

A Little Simple Math... Or So You May Think

So let's assume the best possible scenario. You went to the store and sold twenty shirts for ten dollars each. Let' assume the shirts cost you only five dollars each, so naturally you made five dollars on each shirt.

What's that? A hundred dollars! You made a profit! Right? Go back to the formula and let's see:

Sales	200$ *(20 shirts x 10$)*
Cost Of Sales	100$ *(20 shirts x 5$)*
Gross Profit	100$

Well, in a perfect world, that's your profit... assuming the order simply fell in your lap. But let's look at a truer depiction of cost of sales. Suppose you had flown to the appointment. What's your profit then? It may look a bit more like this:

Sales		$200
Cost of Sales		
	Shirt Cost	$100
	Airfare	$350
	Transportation	$65
	Hotel	$125

	Food	$75
Total Cost of Sales		$715
Gross Profit (Loss)		($515)

In accounting, a number inside parentheses and/or written in red means it is a negative value; thus, you would have shown a loss of ($515). This is why it is so important to know your *true* cost of sales. When you originally congratulated yourself on making $100, you had actually lost over five hundred. This happens in large companies and small companies alike. The only difference is the losses are normally much bigger in large corporations because the stakes are so much higher. A five hundred dollar loss to a small start-up company, however, can hurt as much, if not more, than a fifty million dollar loss to a large company. This is because large companies, more than likely, have emergency credit lines in place as well as untapped cash reserves that give it the **ability to take a hit**, whereas the small start-up can crumble and fall if even given a simple love-tap.

The Importance Of Counting Pencils

The ability to take a hit is something every company should build into their capital requests when starting a business but very few do. The previous example, however, is a very simple example but it gets much more complicated. Knowing your cost of sales gets even trickier the bigger you get.

What invariably baffles companies is when they consistently have met their projections or even superseded them, but instead of having the twenty-percent profit they had expected, show losses and don't know why. The answer to the *why* is in their interpretation of the cost of sales... and their failure to use the right calculator.

This is the final and most important step in structuring a realistic business model. **Know your cost of sales**. If you've ever worked for a large corporation, you probably noticed a lot of things going on around you that you didn't even think of twice. Employees overusing the phones for personal use; taking supplies home like paper, paper clips, pens, and pencils; using the faxes after hours; using the company FedEx account or messenger service to deliver non-office related packages, etc. Though most don't even take notice, this is why employers cringe every time they witness this happen. It is usually right around then that that familiar *interoffice memorandum* circulates around the office, threatening all the employees for the last time to not take advantage of these resources in the future.

While this can often be a small dent in a rather large corporation, these little expenses can literally destroy a small to mid-sized company. Ross Perot, one of the world's wealthiest people, was once asked the key to his success. He responded that, while he normally had no problem writing the big checks (he knew what they were), he spent countless hours reviewing the smallest... all the way down to the money being spent on pencils. His reasoning was that, most of the time, the big checks are easily justified but the little ones are often where all the frivolous spending takes place and can make the difference between having a healthy company and facing the judge in bankruptcy court.

So what are you supposed to do? Count pencils? Believe it or not, some people do, but that is not what I am suggesting. There are a few things, however, that can be done that can greatly help cut down costs in these areas.

First, **lock the office supply drawers** and designate one person responsible for its disbursement. This includes not only pens, pencils, and paper, but also tape, envelopes, stamps, hole punchers and other things that can be taken home and used for personal use. Especially stamps, that's a big one.

Second, and of even greater consequences, run a tight reign on **overnight shipping** and **messenger services**. Have a log that every employee must fill out when using these services, and have it required that it must be approved *before* and not after the package is shipped. So many companies are shocked when they see these bills at the end of the period and then proceed to start slapping wrists. This doesn't work because the damage has already been done and, most of the time, the pattern will repeat itself again because if they got away with it the first time, they believe that they'll get away with it again.

Third, and possibly most important is to set up a **password phone system** that requires individual passwords for outgoing service. This way, each person is responsible for his or her calls each month and there is no way to hide the fact that they made the call. Once you assign passwords, tell each person they are responsible for their own password, and it is their responsibility not to tell anyone else their password, so no one can blame someone else for using their password other than themselves.

Looking Even Closer At Costs

Let's take a closer look at a more realistic example of cost of sales...

By now you have probably gained a pretty good sense of the importance of knowing your cost of sales. I truly believe that getting a grip on cost of sales is a key to the success of most businesses. Thus far, I have shown the most basic formula of *sales - cost of sales = gross profit*, and have shown an example how such a simple formula can be miscalculated so easily, as in my example of losing $515 when it was originally thought a profit of $100 had been made.

So let's look at a real example, to show you how tremendously complicated the equation really is, and how the Murphy button actually works in action...

As you learned from the previous example, the cost of sales goes beyond simply the cost of the shirt itself, but includes everything else that was done along the way to get to that point. Expenses within the cost of sales can be broken down into two parts. The first part is the expenses that are constant and recurring in your everyday business. These costs are normally referred to as your *overhead* also called *general & administrative costs (G&A)*. The other part consists of the expenses that are variable and change as your business grows (or declines). These are called *variable* costs. They normally become less when your company has lower revenue, and higher when your revenue is up, thus these expenses can be normally kept in balance.

Your overhead, on the other hand, cannot be easily controlled, as they consist of the expenses required to keep your company running on a day-to-day basis, so your cash flow or capital reserves must always *at the very least* match these costs *no matter what.* Out of control overhead kills businesses. Every company must make sure it has the cash flow necessary to cover its overhead. If you are a startup, you need enough startup capital to cover overhead until your company has its own cash flow to support these expenses.

It should be clear to you from the outset how much cash flow your business must have to keep things running. This is known as the company's breakeven and is a function of a minimum number of units sold given a specific cost of sales and the recurring overhead costs. More simply put, you need to know how much you need to ship in order to pay your bills! If you are a service-driven business, you need to know how much client and/or customer revenue needs to come in to cover your expenses.

When you are starting a business, it is also imperative that you know the average time it takes in your industry for a business to earn a return on investment so you know how much start-up capital you need until your company is making money and starts to pay back investors. This is a guideline you must follow to give your company the best chance of succeeding before running out of money and forcing you to jump into the classifieds for a new line of work.

In my company, I estimated I needed three years of overhead in my initial capital offering, since the average return on investment in my industry was a minimum of three years. So what does your overhead consist of? Let's take a look at some of the expenses...

Salaries
Rent
Telephone
Utilities
Health Insurance
Priority Shipping
Office Supplies
Travel
Professional Fees
Web site Maintenance
Postage

These expenses in your overhead are your company's lifeline and are absolutely necessary for your company to stay in existence. It is important to understand however, that a company's set overhead does increase from time to time as new people are hired and a company's needs grow; however, any new overhead costs can be quickly calculated as they will tend to remain stable until the next growth spurt happens and the overhead has to be reset again.

So what are the variable expenses? These are expenses that change constantly or often enough to separate from your fixed cost or overhead. For example, if sales change for the greater (or worse), more (or less) money is going to be paid to salespersons that are working on commissions. Also, increasing (or decreasing) seasonal demand (if one season is generally busier than another) has to always be taken into account to make sure you have enough money set aside to manage these growth spurts or down times. In my business, the fall season was twice as busy as the spring, so I needed to make sure I saved enough money from the fall, to get through the lean season that always followed. Let's take a look at a list of variable expenses...

These expenses vary and increase and decrease proportionally depending upon your company revenues. For example, if one season, you have $1 million in orders, your variable costs may look like this...

Sales		**$1,000,000**
Inventory		*$500,000*
Marketing Budget		
Advertising	$35,000	
Product Giveaways	$10,000	
Posters/Stickers	$ 5,000	
Total Marketing Budget		$50,000
Selling Expenses		
Sales Commissions	$50,000	
Store Giveaways	$20,000	
Total Selling Expenses		*$70,000*
Sales Profit Margin		$380,000

Overhead (G&A)		$200,000
Gross Operating Profits		$180,000

If your company writes $3 million dollars in orders the following season, the numbers will naturally increase accordingly, as more inventory needs to be brought in, more marketing needs to be done to support the increase, and so forth and so on. Typically, your company should always run off formulas and percentages. For example, in my market, the formula went as follows. Remember, all these percentages are percentages of sales (which represent the 100%):

Sales		**100%**
Variable Costs		
Cost of Inventory	50%	
Marketing	5%	
Sales Commissions	7%	
Overhead (G&A)	20%	
Gross Operating Profit		18%

If you are reading this and happen to have some accounting experience, you will notice I am giving an extremely basic and simple approach to the accounting. The actual representations happen to be quite a bit more complex and different from this format, but believe me, the principle is the same and my goal is to make you understand this, and not confuse you by it.

There's a key flaw to this formula however, if you are starting a business. In fact, you can throw the whole thing out. The above formulas are a perfect guide to follow (in my particular market) if and only if you are at a point of sales maximization. What the hell is sales maximization? Let me explain...

Sales Maximization

When you did all your research on all the competitors in your market, you probably found a common formula similar to the one above. But there's one problem. It goes back to that step of **knowing where you are**. Though these formulas are great to go by, when you start a business, you have virtually no sales, so all the percentages mean nothing. Most of the time in a start-up, your yearly overhead is more than your first year's sales. That is a fact. Is that a bad thing? Not at all!

Remember that it takes money to make money. As your company grows, it comes closer and closer until it reaches the point that it is running close to the formula above (or whatever your market's formula may be). That is what is called the point of sales maximization. For example, your marketing expenses may be as much as three hundred percent of your first year's sales, seventy percent of your second year's sales before leveling off at where it needs to be between five and eight percent by year three or four. The same applies to your cost of inventory. The factory may charge you 90% of your actual sale price in your first year, 70% percent in your second year (as your volume increases), before leveling off at 40-45% percent when reaching the point of sales maximization.

6 Questions To Be Prepared For

Hopefully, you are beginning to see that you must give your company enough time to both reach the point of sales maximization, and pick a conservative and realistic time period to expect a return on investment, as that question will invariably be one of the first questions that any investor will ask from the onset. Typically, there are six basic questions asked from the beginning.

1. What type of money are you looking for?
2. Are you looking for a debt and/or equity investment?
3. (If equity), how much equity are you prepared to offer for the money you are looking for?
4. (If debt) what percent interest are you expecting to pay for the loan?
5. What and when is your projected return on investment?
6. How will my money be spent (use of proceeds)?

Recap

So, let's recap for a moment to make sure you have soaked in the above points...

You've figured out that the research you had done on all the companies in your market reflects formulas, numbers, and percentages that are different from the formulas, numbers, and percentages of your company when it is a start-up.

You have learned that, because of this, the difference in both formulas and numbers reflect the amount of money you need in start-up capital, as your company cannot and will not make any money until you get to that point.

You have also learned that point is referred to as your point of sales maximization, and that point is the barometer for your company, gauging when it will start to make money.

You have learned the difference between start-up, variable, and fixed costs (overhead), and that any of the three, if left unmanaged, can put you in a world of hurt.

You have also learned that the start-up numbers, if managed properly, hopefully begin looking like the sales maximization numbers, the closer and closer you come to the time you estimated for your return on investment.

Let's take it a few steps further...

Return on Investment

Planning the return on investment is a big job and you should receive as much guidance as you can before saying the magic number. Let me explain...

In my market, the projected return on investment was three to five years from **minimum or maximum capitalization**. Minimum or maximum capitalization is the least and most (respectively) money required to release the investment to your company. In other words, when you are looking for an investment of money into your company, you usually set a minimum amount (minimum capitalization) and a maximum amount (maximum capitalization) required in order for the investment to take place. This is often mandatory in investments made through Private Placement Memorandums (mentioned earlier), as it protects investors from making a bad investment. Let me explain...

Suppose you are looking for a minimum capitalization of $1 million dollars. To do this, you may be looking for ten to twenty people to invest between fifty thousand and one hundred thousand dollars apiece. You show them all the numbers they need and what a million dollars would do for your company, how the money would be used, etc.

Minimum capitalization protects the investors that jumped in first from releasing their money until the minimum capitalization is reached. All combined investments that still fall short of a million dollars are held in an escrow account until minimum capitalization is reached. Why is this? Let's go further...

Remember, the only reason why these investors have chosen to invest is because they believe in your cumulative plan. You have explained how you believe one million dollars would help you achieve certain milestones. This does not mean if you receive 80% the amount, your investors expect you to accomplish 80% of what you said you would do. That's not how it works. The minimum capitalization is all or none. If you don't reach it, not one penny will be released.

That being said, let's say you have only managed to get five people to put in fifty thousand dollars each. This means you only have a quarter of what you were looking for.

Your obligation at this point is three fold. You can, leave the money in escrow in hopes to reach the minimum capitalization, you can give the money back to the investors, or you can set up a meeting between the five people that invested and ask them if they are willing to agree to reset the minimum capitalization point to two hundred and fifty thousand, rather than the million dollars you were originally seeking.

The third situation will rarely happen if you are so far away from the original number like in this example, and will normally only be agreed upon, if you were at eight or nine hundred thousand and were close enough to justify the investment. In this case, a savvy move would be to encourage the five investors to increase their initial investments to meet a new agreed upon minimum capitalization point based on a new plan you develop reflecting those numbers to show how this lesser amount will still work. This would allow the business to commence, albeit under possibly slightly different terms than was originally planned.

Setting the **time period** on your return on investment is often equally as important as getting the investment itself, as, if you set the time too soon, you have the potential to either create hostile investors and/or leave your company with no cash reserves when the market goes through its dips, as every company has their peaks and valleys.

Furthermore, you have to tell your investors up front not only when you plan to start paying them, but how much and how often, as well. Here are some basic guidelines to making the right decisions, and an example of how the Murphy button works in action.

The Murphy Button

First, if you have done your research, and it has shown the typical return on investment is three to five years, decide if you are willing to accept nothing less than the latter, five years... at the minimum. Why? If three years is best-case scenario, and five years is worst-case scenario, Murphy's scenario is at least seven or eight, so going less than five is suicide.

Second, remember that estimating the return on investment is heavily dependent upon your sales projections, so make sure your sales projections are

conservative and *realistic*. Once you determine your realistic projections, hit the Murphy button. This will automatically cut that number by *a third* and give you the projection to go with. Once you have done your research, and picked conservative sales projections, you should be able to figure out how long it will take you to reach the point of sales maximization... and make that point extremely conservative and realistic as well. Once you estimate the point of sales maximization, it is then that you should start making money, so naturally, that is when you begin paying back the investors, right? *Wrong.*

This is the point where you start creating some value in your company. The red ink turns black, arbitrary and blue-sky value becomes book value, equipment or inventory is purchased, long-term debts become capital assets, and your company starts planning for the growth spurts of the future.

Do this as long as you can until you feel you have the reserves to get through the peaks and valleys of the future (remember that peaks require more money too). At the very point you think you are ready to pay dividends, hit the Murphy button again. That will add about six months or so to the clock before such payoffs are scheduled to take place. If your investors are smart, they will know that the more money your company reinvests in itself, the healthier the company, and the more money everyone will make in the future. If they take out the money too soon, the whole ship can go down very quickly.

Also, remember to hit the Murphy button after every cost-of-sales entry. This will increase every estimated cost ten percent from what you have projected.

So what have you done? First, your sales projections are decreased by a third. Second, you will increase the cushion of your return on investment by an additional ten to twenty percent and, third, your estimated cost of sales will increase by ten percent to bring you much closer to your true profit if and when such a point takes place.

So what happens if you actually hit the sales, cost of sales, and profit numbers you had originally estimated as well as the projected return on investment time period without using the button? Then, you're a hero. This is a perfect example of managing expectations or the under-promise and over-deliver example we spoke about in the previous chapters.

Your Accountant Is Your Doctor

The final thing you must understand is the value of your accountant. I cannot emphasize this point enough. Put simply, your accountant is the doctor of your business, and the proper business guidance at this time is mandatory, as your accountant should be able to diagnose the health of your company a heck of a lot better and more precisely than you. Just as you go to the doctor every three months or so for a check-up, never miss your quarterly check-up with your accountant as, like a doctor, he will both check the overall health of your company, and tell you what to do until you see him the next time.

...And make sure he uses the right calculator.

11

WISHING YOU A SAFE AND ENJOYABLE JOURNEY...

It is no accident that this book ends in Chapter 11. If you are perceptive enough to already recognize why this is please bare with me...

According to current statistics kept by the U.S. Small Business Administration, there are about 29 million small businesses in the U.S. Each year about 10-12 percent additional new firms with employees open and each year about 10-12 percent of small businesses that are started by ambitious and determined entrepreneurs eventually file for bankruptcy protection (Chapter 11), or just cease operations and close their doors. The reasons for failure are one or some combination of the following:

- Lack of experience
- Insufficient capital (money)
- Poor location
- Poor inventory management
- Over-investment in fixed assets
- Poor credit arrangement management
- Personal use of business funds
- Unexpected growth

About half of all new establishments survive five years or more and about one third survive 10 years or more. As one would expect, the probability of survival increases with a firm's age.

Failure, I hope you have already discerned from my experiences, does not mean "*The End*" and/or that it is all over for you. Failure happens to everyone starting out. Succeeding in business is about losing the battles but eventually winning the war. Most who fail learn, retool and start again, this time a bit wiser and considerably more well informed than before. Some of the world's richest and most successful and powerful businessmen have all experienced it, some multiple times.

• • • • •

Carl Icahn who is reported to be worth $20.3 billion by Forbes, filed for corporate bankruptcy in 1991 when he owned, and subsequentially lost, TWA (Trans World Airlines) to his creditors.

Donald Trump, who is reported to be worth $2.7 billion by Forbes, has filed for *corporate* bankruptcy four (that's right 4) times, in 1991, 1992, 2004 and 2009. All of these bankruptcies involved over-leveraged casino and hotel properties.

• • • • •

If you learn anything at all from this reading experience, know this: Even if *"failure"* is not an option, it is a path you must take on the road to recurring and sustainable success.

A Few Last Words...

That's pretty much it! Before I leave you, however, let me say a few final words of advice...

In my life, I've been broke and happy, and I've been rich and miserable, and I promise you, broke and happy wins every time. If you combine the two however, and become rich (for lack of a better word) and happy, it's your best bet, as fortunately or unfortunately, we live in a Western society that provides you with more access to enjoyment the deeper and more lined your pockets become. That is a shameless fact.

Here's another fact...if you love your work you're not working, that is key. Appreciate the journey, keep record of your progress and enjoy it the whole way through. I know this is easier said than done, but nothing in life worth anything comes easy. The years that I missed while obsessing with my business, I now realize that I can never get back, and it truly hurts. I missed my Dad's surprise 60th birthday party, I missed my nephew being born, I missed visiting my Grandfather to play chess before he passed, I remember my Mom crying when I forgot Mother's day, I missed annual ski trips with my family, all my friends weddings... you name it, I missed it... and I thoroughly regret it.

Know that the life of an entrepreneur is extremely difficult. Among the obvious reasons this is true is the fact that you work for an extremely stubborn and bull-headed person (yourself), as evidenced by what is willingly sacrificed to succeed. That being said, you must find a balance if you plan to succeed... or die in the process, as I have witnessed countless "successful" entrepreneurs smoke, drink, and stress themselves to death and all I can think of is... what exactly was the point? Was it worth it?

Luckily, I caught myself just in time... At least I think I did.

Good luck in your journey, be happy and confident with each and every step you take ... and watch out for the snakes that you will come across along the way.

HELPFUL LINKS & RESOURCES

N2ITIV is a blog that Gary and I created where we share hundreds of articles, videos, and training modules on what we think are the most important lessons we have learned from our entrepreneurial experiences. Here is a guide and a series of links that may be of value as you take your journey.

Branding

Gary and I have spent over 45 years combined handling the branding for four companies which we have owned together, as well as for some of the top brands and entertainment personalities in the world. If you want to catch up on all branding posts, click http://www.n2itivsolutions.com/category/brand-strategy/.

How To Raise Money To Start A Business

I have also written a number of articles on the subject of raising capital and pursuing investors. I have been on both sides of the table as well as in the middle quite a few times so I have an interesting perspective and decent insight on the subject I think. If you want to read those articles, http://www.n2itivsolutions. com/category/startups/.

Help For New Businesses

If you are starting a business, there is a section you should not miss, as it will give you access to 4 training modules that Gary and I spent quite a bit of time on. It is called The Start-Up Toolkit. A lot of people contact Gary and I and ask us questions that we have already answered in detail in those videos. To find out about The Start-Up Toolkit, click http://www.n2itivsolutions.com/start-up-toolbox-2/

Business Strategy Tips

There is another cool section on the blog that contains short video modules offering business tips that you can implement in your business to help you. It is called the Bear Essentials. To access it click http://www.n2itivsolutions.com/bear-essentials/

For The Entrepreneur

We have developed a section specifically with the entrepreneur in mind. This area of our blog highlights a lot of the challenges we have faced as entrepreneurs and what we have learned in our experiences along the way that may be of help to you. To access this section click http://www.n2itivsolutions.com/category/entrepreneur/

Success Tips & Advice

One of the biggest portions of the N2ITIV blog contains stories of success and various tips and advice on how to be successful in your business affairs, whether you work for yourself, or somebody else. If that is more your speed, click http://www.n2itivsolutions.com/category/success-2/

Videos

If videos are more your speed, we have tons of videos on this site as well. To watch videos, instead of reading text, by all means, click http://www.n2itivsolutions.com/category/video/

Good luck!

ABOUT THE AUTHOR

MJ GOTTLIEB is a lifelong entrepreneur, having owned and operated five businesses and one not-for profit foundation over the last 23 years. He is *the co-owner of The N2ITIV Group, Inc., a strategic consulting firm specializing in the implementation of creative business strategies to help aspiring entrepreneurs and small businesses* increase their brand awareness and monetize their businesses.

MJ's expertise focuses on five principal areas: start-up development, corporate strategy, brand management/licensing, conceptualization and implementation of product launches, and helping start-ups to create strategic alliances to help fund their growth. *He writes regularly on his blog, www.n2itivsolutions.com.*

About The Illustrator

William Roth, age 12, lives with his two dogs, two cats, and two parents in New Jersey, where he is a seventh grader in middle school. This is the first book he has illustrated. He sold his first pictures at age 6—to a toy company—and received his first commission -- to paint a mural in a child's bedroom—at age 9. He often draws pictures for his friends, and it was his friend Emery who introduced him to MJ Gottlieb

CPSIA information can be obtained at www.ICGtesting.com
Printed in the USA
BVOW04s1040231016

465523BV00009B/5/P